FOR CHRIST'S SAKE

TOM HARPUR

FOR CHRIST'S SAKE

McCLELLAND & STEWART

First published by Oxford University Press, 1986
This edition published by McClelland & Stewart, 1993

Library and Archives Canada Cataloguing in Publication

Harpur, Tom
    For Christ's sake

ISBN 13: 978-0-7710-3945-4
ISBN 10: 0-7710-3945-X

1. Jesus Christ – Historicity.   2. Jesus Christ – Biography.
3. Jesus Christ – Teachings.
I. Title

BT303.2.H37 1993   232.9'08   C93-094189-6

We acknowledge the financial support of the Government of Canada
through the Book Publishing Industry Development Program and
that of the Government of Ontario through the Ontario Media
Development Corporation's Ontario Book Initiative. We further
acknowledge the support of the Canada Council for the Arts and
the Ontario Arts Council for our publishing program.

Printed and bound in Canada
The paper used in this book is acid-free.

McClelland & Stewart Ltd.
75 Sherbourne Street
Toronto, Ontario
M5A 2P9
www.mcclelland.com

3 4 5 6 7   10 09 08 07 06

For the Countess

"Love is her greatest gift by far
And all her ways are peace."

CONTENTS

PREFACE

I am very pleased to have the opportunity of writing this introduction to the new, McClelland & Stewart edition of *For Christ's Sake*. This edition, with its cleaner, larger print and its much more relevant cover, is a form of literary resurrection. It combines two essentials that Christianity has always held to be true of each individual's personal resurrection one day—transformation simultaneous with recognizeable continuity! In addition, it brings me a special pleasure because it affords me the privilege, not often experienced by a writer, of being able to set my original work in a fresh and much wider context.

Before going further, however, I would like to caution the reader. This book is not for those who are "at ease in Zion." In other words, it is not intended for those who are completely comfortable with the traditional version of the Christian faith and who have no intention of putting themselves through the pain of what the experts call cognitive dissonance, that is, the angst of entertaining new ideas. Those who feel no doubts, suffer no anxieties and hold no fears about the nature and the communication of the orthodox positions of the Church in the dying years of this millennium should read no further. I have no wish to upset anyone who would rather not be disturbed intellectually.

Since the spring of 1986, when *For Christ's Sake* first appeared, causing a burst of controversy, much has happened—to the world itself, to the religious scene (particularly the study of who Jesus is and the nature of his mission) and, finally, to the book. I would like to comment briefly on each of these three dimensions, in reverse order:

The Book: *For Christ's Sake* touched off a keen and at times acrimonious debate across Canada within days of its publication in mid-February 1986. It went into a third printing less than six weeks later and has now sold more than 30,000 copies to make it one of the best-selling books on religion by a Canadian. (Pierre Berton's *The Comfortable Pew*, which was commissioned by the Anglican Church of Canada and published by McClelland & Stewart in 1965, holds the record at 139,000). In 1987, Huntington College of Laurentian University created a seven-part series of thirty-minute television programs, also called *For Christ's Sake*, which featured conversations with me about the book's major themes. The programs were made for use in the college's extension work throughout the North, and subsequently videos were made available for church study groups. When Vision/TV, the world's first interfaith television network went on the air in 1988, they obtained a license for the series and have broadcast it from coast to coast to more than five million cable subscribers several times. The license was renewed in 1992 by Vision, and so it will be aired again from time to time over the coming months and years.*

During the tumultuous weeks following its first appearance, the book was praised by many as a liberating breath of fresh air and criticized by others as an arrogant and flagrant example of heresy. A vigorous group of fundamentalists on the West Coast, mainly in and around Surrey, B.C., waged a strident, long-distance telephone campaign to have me dismissed both from *The Toronto Star*, where I have been a freelance columnist on religion and ethics since 1984, and from The Toronto School of Theology, where I was for five years a part-time lecturer on the theology and praxis of mass media. Other ministers, for example, a Salvation Army leader in Owen Sound, Ontario, took out advertisements in their local newspapers announcing sermons and lectures denouncing the book and my main thesis that Jesus was not a Christian. Most of the ultra-conservative Christian bookstores refused to carry it—or any of my subsequent books.

There was a barrage of letters to the editors of many newspapers, and many were printed, even ones that took up an entire page in the weekend religion sections. Religious publications and most major newspapers carried reviews and sometimes a news story as well. *The Canadian Jewish News*, which later attacked me for my views on kosher killing (see *God Help Us*, M&S, 1992) ran two favorable reviews by distinguished rabbis. Interviews on "Morningside" and many other key radio and television talk shows, together with the other publicity, spawned a flood of personal mail. It still comes in and has remained overwhelmingly positive over the years. But there has been considerable vitriol as well. Hell hath no fury like religious people who have been forced to rethink their deepest beliefs—or prejudices.

As hinted already, though, the most characteristic reaction from Church people and outsiders alike has been: "Thanks for speaking out; it's what I've vaguely felt for years but could never express properly." Many, from all walks of life and from a kaleidoscope of denominational backgrounds—as well as none—have said they never would have lapsed from their churches if such a view of Jesus' life and teaching had been available to them years ago. The response from young people, especially those at university, has been most gratifying of all. Except, that is, for the theologian at one of our largest Roman Catholic colleges who phoned after hearing an interview about *For Christ's Sake* on CBC's religious radio show, "Open House," to say that he was telling all his students—some of them future seminarians—to read it. He said: "You have written what most of us would like to be able to say aloud but cannot for fear of being forbidden to teach at all."

Some theologians who agreed with my chief conclusions felt the book should have been much longer. And I agree, it could have been a much larger tome. The subject is huge and the issues raised are of extreme importance. But, over the years I have seen numerous thick, scholarly works on Jesus appear only to languish largely unread in theological libraries. I wanted the book to be read by as many people as possible and so I deliberately kept it short. If anyone thinks this made the task easier I should point out that it's infinitely harder to say what you mean and have it understood in a short space than a long. As the man who was suddenly asked to give a speech said: "When do you want it and how long should it be? If you want me to talk for ten minutes, I won't be ready until tomorrow. If you want me to talk for an hour, I'm ready right now."

Books on Jesus: There has been a spate of books since 1986, and especially in the past year or so. This is neither the time nor place to enter into a detailed review of any of them. But two things have impressed me about this phenomenon. Interest in Jesus Christ has never been greater. Yet, looking at most of the recent offerings, it seems as though the various authors are striving to outdo one another in their imaginative and occasionally—as with Gore Vidal's 1992 book, *Live from Golgotha*—offensive scenarios. Overall, the tone is negative and reductionist. Jesus is, at best, just another "great guy," a prophet or itinerant philosopher who met an untimely end. The British biographer A. N. Wilson's *Jesus: A Life*, published in 1992, is a disappointing rationalization of the author's own unbelief. But what has bothered me most about the bulk of the recent Jesus books, however, is the near-total lack of biblical evidence for some of the theories being advanced—for example, that Jesus had children by Mary Magdalene, who went on to constitute the "Grail" of royal blood in Europe, or that he was the "Teacher of Righteousness" mentioned in the Dead Sea Scrolls.

The scrolls themselves, especially now that the remaining manuscripts are being quickly made public, have helped to fuel the renewed speculation about Jesus and about the origins of Christianity in general. Here again, however, it must be said that while the scrolls tell us a tremendous amount about Judaism just before and at the time of Christ, they reveal very little that directly changes how we think about this pivotal figure. John the Baptist may well have belonged for a time to the Qumran community, the source of the scrolls, situated at the north end of the Dead Sea, but its influence on Jesus is minimal, at least in the light of those scrolls published to date. The most significant development since 1986 in this regard has been the discovery of the title "Son of God" in one of the Qumran papyri used in relation to a person other than Jesus. As far as *For Christ's Sake* is concerned, this simply reinforces the argument made there that to be called the Son of God in a Jewish setting in the first century is not by any means the same thing as being identical with God Himself.

The idea that the Vatican has been suppressing the publication of the scrolls, as at least one recent popular book has claimed, is patently ridiculous. The long delay has been the result of scholarly rivalries not of church-inspired plots. I should add that I find Barbara Thiering, author of *Jesus and the Riddle of the Dead Sea Scrolls*, also published in 1992, one of the most inventive—and least convincing—Jesus chroniclers of them all. She takes the view that the whole New Testament is really a code in which nothing is what it appears to be. Rather, it is all a series of symbols telling us about what is going on in the Essene community at Qumran. The uninformed public seems to gobble up this kind of dubious scholarship, yet it must be said that "deep down it is very shallow." It reminds me of the ill-fated and thoroughly discredited attempt by the late British professor John Allegro to show that the entire Bible was a code about a cult devoted to a hallucenogenic mushroom! (The publishers actually issued an apology afterwards for having foisted *The Sacred Mushroom and the Cross* upon an unsuspecting public.)

Our Changing World: It has been only seven years since *For Christ's Sake* was first published. Yet in that time the Cold War has ended, the Berlin Wall has come down, Communism has virtually disappeared, and the former superpower, the Soviet Union, has collapsed into an assortment of fractious and nearly bankrupt republics. At the same time there has been a resurgence of militant fundamentalism in most major world religions. But, while Islam and Christianity are still growing rapidly in Africa and other parts of the Third World, the decline in the churches' influence and numbers in the developed countries has continued relentlessly. There are symptoms on every side of the enormous spiritual and ethical vacuum left in the wake of the failure of old creeds to meet the deepest longings of modern men and women. The chief strategy of many Christian groups, namely to keep on saying what they always have said but to do so more loudly, is not working.

For Christ's Sake was originally written not to be controversial nor to disturb the faithful but as an attempt to wrestle anew with the only evidence about Jesus we have, the New Testament. I wanted to see whether its message, compromised and changed over the years to suit a range of political and other interests, could be released anew in terms ordinary people could understand today. In other words, is there good news there for a spiritually confused and empty generation and can it be communicated to young and old alike?

Unlike other, liberal studies of the life of Jesus, *For Christ's Sake* is not slanted by a priori assumptions that anything remotely suggestive of the supernatural or of the miraculous must instantly be dismissed. Indeed, one of the major criticisms of the book made by agnostics, liberals, and others is that it isn't radical enough. My belief in the Resurrection, for example, offends their demand that the Jesus story be reduced to an admirable but nevertheless highly exaggerated, mythical (in a pejorative sense) moralistic tale. Religious conservatives, on the other hand, obviously feel that the book goes much too far. Most of them, of course, have never troubled to read it for themselves. If they did so they would quickly discover that whatever its faults—and I make no claim to have arrived at the final truth about so vast and so complex a matter—*For Christ's Sake* deals not with abstract speculations about Jesus but with what the Greek texts of the Gospels and epistles actually say. Anyone who takes his stand on "what the Bible says" has an obligation at least to take this claim seriously and to check the arguments out for himself.

This is a book about the roots of the Christian faith. It's about breaking through the barriers of dogma and the packaging of dusty traditions to the vision and work of Jesus Christ himself. It's a call not just for some minor updating in modern Christianity but for a radically New Reformation based upon the realization that the Church itself is largely to blame for people's inability to hear and heed the Gospel in our time. Repentance, as the Bible itself says, must begin at "the House of the Lord."

People are spiritually hungry or thirsty today as never before in the modern era. They have not lost their vital interest in spiritual matters just because they do not attend synagogue, temple, or church as often as they or their parents once did. As the vice-president of a leading American publishing house told his staff not long ago, his firm alone currently receives 10,000 book proposals annually for books on religious themes—and has done so for five or six years. That works out to 27.3 manuscripts a day, including Saturdays and Sundays! It's for this reason that I believe *For Christ's Sake* has an urgent relevance today. It attempts to tell the story of Jesus Christ with scriptural integrity, with the best insights modern scholarship can offer, and with an eye on the spiritual questions modern men and women are asking. Even if the book merely provokes readers to think about the Christian good news in ways they never have before it will have accomplished its task.

Finally, for those who have heard it said that this book denies the divinity of Jesus Christ, I want to say this couldn't be more wrong. True, I interpret this divinity, on the basis of the text and in the context of our modern spiritual quest, quite differently than the Church has traditionally done. But this is far from saying Jesus was not the bearer and revealer of the divine. He was, and so, although admittedly to a much lesser degree, are we. Therein lies both our calling and our hope. What I have tried to do is to show that, paradoxically, Jesus' divinity lay in his being fully human. If you believe, as I have attempted to show, that the New Testament's understanding of what it means to be fully human is to have realized one's total potential as a spiritual being, then Jesus was indeed the pioneer and forerunner of this fulfilled kind of humanity. He holds out to us today the challenge and the invitation to follow in his way.

Tom Harpur
Easter, 1993

* *Publisher's Note:* The video tapes for the seven-part series *For Christ's Sake* can be purchased or rented from The Centre for Spirituality and Health, Huntington College, Laurentian University, Ramsey Lake Road, Sudbury, Ont. P3E 2C6 Tel: 1-800-461-6366.

". . . the letter killeth, but the spirit giveth life."
II Corinthians 3:6

PROLOGUE

Anonymous
The Jesus who
Keeps saying "I am Jesus,
'Look at me,
There is no substitute"
Is an imposter. Do not trust
The Christian cult of
Personality. I came
To turn you on and not
To turn you off,
To make you free and not
To tie you up.
My yoke was easy and
My burden light
Until they made
Salvation copyright, and
All in the name of Jesus.
So forget
My name was ever Jesus.
From now on
I am anonymous.
                              Sydney Carter[1]

The Spring of Living Waters: A Parable for Our Time

THERE ARE times when the deepest truths about the human condition can only be told by means of a parable. The bite of such stories does not depend on their being literally or historically factual—for example, the "truth" of Jesus' parable of the prodigal son in no way hinges on the question of whether he was referring to a specific father and son at a specific time. Let us use our imagination, then, and "see" the following:

There was once a vast, rocky wilderness, void of all vegetation but the hardiest thorns and briers. Through the middle of the desert stretched a rough highway along which the whole of humanity was making its pilgrimage. They straggled along footsore and thirsty, tired and frightened by a myriad of nameless fears.

But at one point along the way a clear spring of running water bubbled up out of the naked rock. No one knows who first discovered it; that secret has long since been lost. Yet for countless generations the people journeying along the road stopped to refresh themselves there. And as they did so, they found to their surprise and delight that the waters not only slaked their thirst, but satisfied deeper needs as well. Somehow in drinking at that source they found their minds and bodies healed, their hopes and courage growing strong again. Life became rich with fresh meaning. They found they could pick up their various burdens and take to the way once more with new hearts. They called the spot "the place of living waters" and the spring itself, "the water of life."

Now, as time went on various people began to roll up boulders around the spring as monuments of gratitude. As the generations and centuries passed, these monuments became more elaborate and ornate, until at last the spring was totally enclosed, arched over by a great fortress-like cathedral and protected by high stone walls. A special caste of men, with special robes and a language all their own, came into being to set rules for preserving the purity of the well. Access was no longer free to all, and disagreements as to who could drink there, and when, and how, sometimes grew so bitter that wars were fought over them.

The victors always put up more monuments and safeguards in gratitude for winning, and so it was that, as the years rolled by, the spring itself was bricked over and lost from view. No one remembered when exactly it was done or by whom. But when the pilgrims complained about the loss, and many were found fainting or even near death on the road, those now in charge either mocked their cries or simply ignored them. Beautiful ceremonies were carried out inside the holy place to celebrate what the well had done for pilgrims many years before, while at the very gates people were dying of thirst.

Eventually other water was piped in, at great expense, from distant places, but it seemed a mere shadow compared to the reality that once had been there for all to enjoy. From time to time strange men came in from the wilderness saying that those who guarded the ancient well should "repent" and tear away all the obstructions so that the masses might drink and be restored. Later they would be called prophets and honored greatly in the shrine. But at the moment of their protest they were rejected. Indeed, many were put to death.

And so in the end the vast majority of people who journeyed along that route avoided the now-sacred "place of living waters" and survived whatever way they could. Many, when they passed the shrine and recalled the stories they had learned in youth about the hidden spring, were seized with nostalgia and longings too deep to utter. Others struggled on embittered by cynical doubt that the healing waters had ever existed. But sometimes in the night, when all the chanting and ceremonies were stilled, those few pilgrims who stole into the shrine to rest for a moment in some corner out of sight were sure they could hear an almost miraculous sound. From somewhere deep under the foundations of the great rock structure there came the faint echo of running water. And their eyes would brim with tears.[2]

It is the contention of this book that Jesus had a divine mission to tear away all the blocks and hindrances standing in the way of humanity's thirst for the water of life. He met with the fate that in some form always befalls those who dare to challenge the rigid, tradition-encrusted orthodoxy of the religious and political-economic status quos: the religious and political authorities had him crucified. But after his death it was not long before the spiritual successors to his tormentors found it useful to crown him as King and God. He came declaring by word and deed a message of good news about God's Kingdom on earth. He proclaimed a message of love that was to save us not from sin but from fear. In the hands of the new authorities, however, the medium became the message and, as a result of this distortion, the message itself was largely ignored.

How all this came about is a long, complex story. It represents the triumph of the lust for absolutes over the necessity of ambiguity; of the lust for power over the summons to inner spirituality and the role of servanthood; of the seductions of Greek philosophical abstractions over the concrete, rooted-in-history temper of Jewish thought. Above all, it embodies a signal, though familiar, victory of the cultic and the hierarchical over the charismatic and the spontaneous in religious experience. Just as the Buddha was not a Buddhist (nor Sigmund Freud a Freudian), so too Jesus was not a Christian—at least not as orthodox or fundamentalist Christianity has defined the term.

Jesus is without question the greatest and most influential figure ever to have left a mark on history; today approximately one billion people of every tribe, color, and tongue are called Christians since they are pledged—at least through baptism—to follow him. But a lifetime of observance of and participation in organized religion, together with prayer and much study, has convinced me that Jesus is not only the greatest person to have lived on planet Earth; he is also the most misunderstood.

THE PROBLEM

WHAT FOLLOWS may upset some people, but that is not my intention. This book is aimed at thoughtful members within the fold who are vaguely uneasy about what they believe, and at that great majority of people for whom the Christian faith now makes little sense at all. My chief concern, since first knowing that I was a Christian, has been for those technically "outside." And the Gospels make it clear that this was the main concern of Jesus too.

Just as the nuclear issue is too important to be left to politicians, so the matter of seeking to clarify who Jesus is—and what it means to follow him as a disciple or learner—is too vital to be left to professional theologians and clergy whose dialogues, however learned, are mostly directed towards others in the same field. While attempting to approach complex issues in a scholarly manner, therefore, I have made every effort to speak to ordinary people in terms they can readily grasp. If some of the book seems to be an attack on cherished beliefs, it is intended positively, as with the surgeon who may have to cut in order to promote healing. My hope is that the reader may come to a clearer vision of his or her "Lord" and in so doing find deeper meaning and satisfaction in living the Kingdom of God and working with others to make it a universally experienced reality here "on earth, as it is in heaven."

The Crisis Facing the Christian Church

Christianity may well be thriving in parts of Africa and Asia today, but in the West Christian faith is eroding at an alarming rate. Secular humanism is fast becoming the prevailing "religion" of the Western World.[1] Less than half of the population of the United States attends church regularly now despite the fact that the Christian message is proclaimed more loudly and continuously on the airwaves than in any other place on earth.

While all the mainline churches have suffered drastic losses since the end of World War II, the U.S. Roman Catholic Church has been hardest hit in the past few years. In 1978, in response to a special Gallup Poll, 74% of Catholics said they had been to church in the previous seven-day period. Five years later, the figure stood at 52%. Today it is roughly 46%. Although the Vatican's position on abortion is unequivocally negative, 72% of American Catholic women polled in early 1986 said they would at least consider it as an option and only 10% were absolutely against it in all circumstances. The decline in the ranks of priests and nuns has been catastrophic. In truth, it is no longer accurate to speak of most Western countries as "Christian" since the vast majority of their citizenry has no traditional ties with any religious body whatever. In Canada, fewer than 30% today attend church regularly—compared with about 70% in 1956—and in England and most European countries the overall average is even worse. The Church of England has closed nine hundred parish churches since 1974! Small wonder that theologians and other commentators on the religious scene speak of this age as "the post-Christian Era" and note that the concept of "Christendom" is now obsolete. Add to this the fact that only a small fraction of children and young people now receive any religious instruction whatever, and the prognosis for the year 2000 looks very bleak indeed.

There are many complex reasons for the decline of Christian faith—the dazzling successes of science and technology, the almost universal flight from the land to city life, the takeover by the state of most social agencies previously run by the churches, the bewilderingly varied messages being beamed towards us by the entire range of mass media, and the proliferating host of options confronting us whenever we have leisure time, to name only a few. But there is a much more central problem to be faced. The Church of Jesus Christ claims to have good news for modern men and women. Since fewer and fewer are being turned on by this news, something obviously is very wrong with the way in which it is being put across. There is in fact a devastating failure in communication. And it will not be solved merely by putting more preachers on television or radio. The so-called mainline churches have much to learn about the use of mass media in communicating their message, but no amount of technical sophistication will avail unless the message itself is one that makes sense. If the basic concepts are irrelevant and incomprehensible to a modern audience, and if, worse still, they actually distort the original good news proclaimed by Jesus and recorded in the Gospels, there can be no effective solution to the current crisis. Without a thoroughgoing effort to reexamine Christian roots with a view to promoting a contemporary and accurate understanding of the gospel, all attempts at evangelism are doomed before they start. It is significant in this connection that the apparent resurgence of fundamentalist-evangelical churches is just that: more apparent than real. They are attracting some members from other churches, and they do hold on to their young people better than their liberal counterparts, but their success in reaching those truly "outside" the faith has been minimal.[2] Similarly, the television evangelists preach to audiences who for the most part are already within their particular fold of beliefs. They solicit money to reach the "unsaved," but scarcely anyone from the "unsaved" community is listening. When the latter do tune in, it's often more from a desire to be entertained by the electronic evangelists' antics than from any genuine interest in the rather meager content of their exhibitions.

Put in its bluntest form, the fact is that the Christian Church is doing a very bad job of communicating who Jesus was and is for humanity and what it was he came to do. Most of the traditional language and dogmas about Jesus are simply incomprehensible to a generation that has seen men walking on the moon.

Consider the following passage from the Nicene Creed, which is in regular use in the Eucharistic worship of the Eastern Orthodox, Roman Catholic, and Episcopal churches worldwide:

I believe in one God the Father Almighty, Maker of heaven and earth, And of all things visible and invisible:

And in one Lord Jesus Christ, the only-begotten Son of God; Light of Light; Very God of very God; Begotten, not made; Being of one substance with the Father; Through whom all things were made: Who for us men and for our salvation came down from heaven, and was incarnate by the Virgin Mary, And was made man, And was crucified also for us under Pontius Pilate. He suffered and was buried, And the third day he rose again according to the Scriptures, And ascended into heaven, And sitteth on the right hand of the Father. . . .

Some people may be able to make sense of this statement of core beliefs, but I cannot—at least not in any ordinary, literal sense of the words and concepts used. And I am certainly far from alone in this.

The problem can be seen in an extreme form in the Creed of St. Athanasius, which still features in Anglican worship and has been widely used in other Western churches since its composition by an unknown author about A.D. 400. The repetitions are tedious and the convolutions of language confusing, to say the least. But I will set it out here so that readers can see for themselves what we are talking about:

Whosoever would be saved needeth before all things to hold fast the Catholic faith.

Which Faith except a man keep whole and undefiled without doubt he will perish eternally.

Now the Catholic Faith is this, that we worship one God in Trinity, and the Trinity in unity;

Neither confusing the Persons nor dividing the substance.

For there is one Person of the Father, another of the Son, another of the Holy Ghost;

But the Godhead of the Father, and of the Son, and of the Holy Ghost is all one, the glory equal, the majesty co-eternal.

Such as the Father is, such is the Son, and such is the Holy Ghost;

The Father uncreated, the Son uncreated, the Holy Ghost uncreated;

The Father infinite, the Son infinite, the Holy Ghost infinite;

The Father eternal, the Son eternal, the Holy Ghost eternal;

Yet there are not three eternals, but one eternal;

As also there are not three uncreated, nor three infinites, but one infinite and one uncreated.

So likewise the Father is almighty, the Son almighty, the Holy Ghost almighty;

And yet there are not three almighties, but one almighty.

So the Father is God, the Son God, the Holy Ghost God;

And yet there are not three Gods but one God.

So the Father is Lord, the Son Lord, the Holy Ghost Lord;

And yet there are not three Lords, but one Lord.

For like as we are compelled by the Christian verity to confess each Person by himself to be both God and Lord;

So we are forbidden by the Catholic religion to speak of three Gods or three Lords.

The Father is made of none, nor created, nor begotten.

The Son is of the Father alone; not made, nor created, but begotten.

The Holy Ghost is of the Father and the Son; not made, nor created, nor begotten, but proceeding.

There is therefore one Father, not three Fathers; one Son, not three Sons; one Holy Ghost, not three Holy Ghosts.

And in this Trinity there is no before or after, nor greater or less;

But all three Persons are co-eternal together, and co-equal.

So that in all ways, as is aforesaid, both the Trinity is to be worshipped in Unity, and the Unity in Trinity.

He therefore that would be saved, let him think thus of the Trinity.

Furthermore, it is necessary to eternal salvation, that he also believe faithfully in Incarnation of our Lord Jesus Christ.

Now the right Faith is that we believe and confess that our Lord Jesus Christ, the Son of God, is both God and Man.

He is God, of the Substance of the Father, begotten before the worlds; and he is Man, of the Substance of his Mother, born in the world;

Perfect God; perfect Man, of reasoning soul and human flesh subsisting;

Equal to the Father as touching his Godhead; less than the Father as touching his Manhood.

Who although he be God and Man, yet he is not two, but is one Christ;

One, however, not by conversion of his Godhead into flesh, but by taking of Manhood into God;

One altogether; not by confusion of Substance, but by unity of Person.

For as reasoning soul and flesh is one man, so God and Man is one Christ;

Who suffered for our salvation, descended into hell, rose again from the dead;

Ascended into heaven, sat down at the right hand of the Father, from whence he shall come to judge the quick and the dead.

At whose coming all men must rise again with their bodies, and shall give account for their deeds.

And they that have done good will go into life eternal; they that have done evil into eternal fire.

This is the Catholic Faith, which except a man do faithfully and steadfastly believe, he cannot be saved.

Book of Common Prayer (CANADA)

Not long ago, I was discussing the much simpler Apostles' Creed with a man who has been a devout and loyal churchman for more than sixty years.[3] He has served as a sidesman and as churchwarden in one of the largest Anglican cathedrals in Canada, always standing at a crisp attention whenever the creeds are said or sung. I asked him how much of it he really understood. "Precious little, if anything," he replied.

In fact, very few preachers can give a reasonable account of either the doctrine of the Trinity or the doctrine of the Incarnation, that is, that Jesus was truly human and yet fully God. They repeat formulae that were worked out, with much quarreling and bitterness, in the fourth and fifth centuries by men whose needs, outlook, and understanding of the universe were vastly different from our own. These formulae are no longer useful—instead, they raise an insurmountable barrier for many who might otherwise become disciples of Jesus in our day.

What is most embarrassing for the Church is the difficulty of proving any of these statements of dogma from the New Testament documents. You simply cannot find the doctrine of the Trinity set out anywhere in the Bible. St. Paul has the highest view of Jesus' role and person, but nowhere does he call him God.[4] Nor does Jesus himself anywhere explicitly claim to be the Second Person of the Trinity, wholly equal to his heavenly Father. As a pious Jew, he would have been shocked and offended by such an idea.

Over the last decade or so, I have talked as long and as frequently as possible about these particular doctrines with intelligent laypeople and clergy of all denominations, and I have found widespread confusion—in itself bad enough. But there is worse to come. This research has led me to believe that the great majority of regular churchgoers are, for all practical purposes, tritheists. That is, they profess to believe in one God, but in reality they worship three. Small wonder Christianity has always had difficulty trying to convert Jews and Muslims. Members of both these faiths have such an abhorrence of anything that runs counter to their monotheism, or faith in the unity of God, that a seemingly polytheistic gospel has little appeal for them.

Since writing the above, I have discussed the Church's problem of making sense out of the traditional God-Man view of Jesus with a senior chaplain at one of Canada's largest hospitals and with the head of one of the oldest and most respected seminaries in the country. Both said orthodox Christianity posed no difficulties for them because they took the whole body of doctrines "symbolically" rather than literally. Asked whether their respective flocks were aware of this, they smiled and shook their heads; the answer was clearly "no." I mention this because it raises the key issue of the gap between clergy and congregation when it comes to matters of faith and dogma. Very few clerics ever pass on what they have learned in theological school about contemporary scholarship on the

Bible—or on anything else, for that matter. Surely it is time for greater honesty from the pulpit.

A Theology of Hostility

As we shall see later, the New Testament provides many different answers to the question, Who is Jesus Christ and what did he come to do? However, for a wide variety of religious, philosophical, and political reasons, what is called by some the absolutist view—Jesus as the pre-existent Lord of creation who comes in human flesh to atone for the sins of the world and then ascends back to glory as the equal of the Father— won out over all the others. It is easy to see why the emperors of the fourth and fifth centuries took a supreme interest in the outcome of the debates over Christology (the technical name for the rational attempt to state who Jesus was and is). Clearly the concept of a divine vice-regent of God, sitting on a heavenly throne, gave ample theological justification for their own earthly panoply of power. It was a useful arrangement that was to last until the final breakup of the Holy Roman Empire. It was the keystone of the edifice known as Christendom. "In Christendom," writes Don Cupitt, University Lecturer in Divinity and Dean of Emmanuel College, Cambridge, "Christ crowned the Emperor, one a step higher in the scale of being merely stooping slightly to bestow authority upon one a step lower. In the Christian iconography [depictions of Christ] . . . to the end of the Byzantine period Christ and the Emperor were virtually indistinguishable. . . . Inevitably Christianity became, or rather was made, absolutist and authoritarian. The Jewishness of Jesus' teaching was lost. . . ."[5]

But the claim by the Church, ever since, that Jesus was fully God while being fully man—"One person in Two Natures which are united unconfusedly, unchangeably, indivisibly, inseparably"[6]—led to other, disastrous consequences. The view that Jesus was God, combined with a literal reading of such Bible passages as "I am the way, the truth, and the life; No man cometh unto the father but by me" meant that God's ultimate and unique self-revelation could be found in Christianity alone. If that was so, all other faiths and religions must

be at best dreadfully incomplete, at worst mere pagan super-
stitions, a fabric of delusion. This explains, although it can
never excuse, the appalling intolerance and violence perpetrated down the centuries against those outside the Christian
fold. The horrors of the Crusades and the notorious Inquisition are but a small part of this tragic tale. Though it has
taken decades since the event, Christian theologians now recognize the full extent of Christian complicity in the Holocaust
of roughly six million Jews by the Nazis. This mind-reeling
attempt at genocide could never have taken place had it not
been for centuries of anti-Semitism fostered by Christian absolutist claims. One has only to read some of Martin Luther's
Table Talk to see how even a spiritual genius could be tainted
by religious intolerance. In 1543 Luther wrote no less than
three lengthy tracts attacking Jews. In *Against the Jews and
Their Lies* he dragged up all the old false rumors—"They poison wells, steal Christian children, whom they torture to ob-
tain their blood"—and went so far as to advocate burning
synagogues, tearing down Jews' houses, seizing their books,
forbidding their rabbis to teach, and forbidding them access
to the public highways. Their gold and silver should be taken
away, he argued, because "they have stolen and robbed us of
it by usury." Because he believed they had rejected Christ, he
became obsessed by the idea of the Jews in his latter years.
"I'd tear their tongues out of their throats," he wrote. "The
Jews, in a word, should not be tolerated. One should neither
eat nor drink with them."[7] It is not a huge mental leap from
this vituperation to the death camps of Belsen and Ausch-
witz.[8]

Many Christians today, especially those of the evangelical
wing, still believe that Jews are there to be converted. Some
even presume to call that tiny group of Jews who have become
Christians "completed Jews." But it is not just a handful of
zealots who hold such a position. The *Book of Common Prayer*
of the Anglican Church of Canada suggests the following special prayer for Good Friday: "O merciful God, who hast made
all men, and hatest nothing that thou hast made, nor wouldest
the death of a sinner, but rather that he should be converted
and live; have mercy upon thine ancient people, and upon all
who reject and deny thy Son; take from them all ignorance,

hardness of heart, and contempt of thy word; and so fetch them home, blessed Lord, to thy fold, that they may be made one flock under one shepherd, Jesus Christ our Lord; who liveth and reigneth with thee and the Holy Spirit, one God, world without end. Amen" (p. 174).

In 1979, in a letter to all his clergy, the then Primate, Most Rev. "Ted" Scott, who was also moderator of the World Council of Churches, requested that this collect be dropped on future Good Fridays. But that such a prayer should exist is a tragic scandal. Instead of seeing other religions as part of the entire story of the human race's continuing struggle for transcendence, or God, the orthodox Christian sees them as fertile fields for the missionary enterprise. It is true that the World Council of Churches has tried to open dialogue between Christians and Muslims, Hindus, Buddhists, Jews, Sikhs, and others, but as fundamentalist protesters at the Vancouver Assembly in 1983 loudly proclaimed, millions of the would-be elect regard this attitude as a sell-out. It is very important to realize, however, that their intolerance of other faiths is in direct proportion to the rigidity of their stance vis-à-vis traditional Christian dogma. Numerous studies of racism and intolerance confirm this assessment. If only the "true believer" is right, then everybody else is wrong, and not only wrong, but a potential enemy.

This kind of absolutism about the claims of Jesus has "legitimized relationships of hostility, isolation, and defensiveness" towards other denominations and other points of view within the Christian Church itself.[9] In other words, a mind-set has been created, an atmosphere in which intolerance of pluralism or differences of any kind seems not merely natural but, at a deeper level, the only course of duty. Here again one may observe the rule: the deeper the commitment to biblical or dogmatic correctness, the stronger the hostility towards other Christians who differ. This tendency accounts for the bitterness with which extremely conservative evangelicals attack the World Council of Churches, and even Billy Graham, for having "fellowship" with liberals and Roman Catholics. But the same kind of mentality is at work in all denominations to some degree, and it is the chief reason why the much-vaunted ecumenical movement is currently grinding to a halt.[10]

A Male Chauvinist Theology

In addition to helping create a theology of hostility, the absolutist view—that Jesus was not a unique agent or messenger sent by God, but himself "very God of very God" come in the flesh—has virtually crowned as monarch a male chauvinist theology. Jesus was obviously male and, so the argument (consciously or unconsciously) goes, if he was also God, then God too must be male. This line of thought lies behind all claims that priets must be male in order to represent Christ properly before his Father and before the people of God.[11]

I have argued elsewhere that Jesus was a radical feminist, breaking most of the anti-female taboos of his day.[12] There is no doubt in my mind that while he used the term "Father" when speaking of God, he did not think of God as a sexual being at all. Some of the parables he told explicitly represent God by a woman. (For example, in Luke 15:8ff., where Jesus tells the parable of the lost coin, the central figure is a woman. In her zealous search for the missing piece of silver, she portrays the love of God for all those lost and alienated from him.) Jesus would have had no difficulty accepting the controversial statement of the ill-fated Pope John Paul I: "It is fitting for us at times to speak of God as our mother." The Old Testament, in fact, does so. The truth of the matter is that even if Jesus was God Incarnate in the traditional sense, his maleness in no way dictates that God as pure being has male sexual attributes. As John's Gospel insists, God is a Spirit and is to be worshipped in spirit and truth. Whatever Jesus' nature was, he had to be either male or female. Had he come at a different time, in different circumstances, he could just as easily have been a woman. It is tempting to speculate on how different the course of Western history might have been if this had been the case. If his followers had stressed the mothering aspect of God's ways with humanity rather than projecting on Him all the aggressive, competitive characteristics so often found in male-dominated societies, would men so readily have been able to invoke His blessing on their wars?

The same day I first typed this passage—May 23, 1984—a headline on the front page of the *Toronto Star* read "God's Male and That's That." The story told how the General Assembly of the Presbyterian Church of Scotland had thrown out a two-year study on the Motherhood of God done by a special task force of seven men and four women. The study stated that God has no gender and that while it would be improper to suggest dropping the use of the word "Father" in prayers, there are ample biblical grounds for using words associated with mothering as well. The assembly, overwhelmingly male, heaped contempt on the whole project (which was only being put forward for study in the denomination's Bible classes) and gave the unmistakable message to the world that in their eyes God is definitely male. Given this kind of archaic and anthropomorphic attitude, it is not surprising that many of the most intelligent women in the various churches have left or are contemplating leaving. Nor is it surprising that religion remains one of the last strongholds of male supremacy in our time.

Summary

Defenders of the traditional orthodoxy about Jesus, including the present Archbishop of Canterbury, Most Rev. Robert Runcie, have a habit of meeting the question of who Jesus was and is with some version of the following proposition: Jesus was either mad or bad, or he was who he claimed to be, the fully divine Son of God, God Himself in-the-flesh. But—quite apart from the matter of whether in fact Jesus did claim to be God—this answer is an unfair way of putting the options. Given a choice between mad, bad, or God, most people would feel forced to opt for the latter. However, there is at least one other alternative. Jesus may have been partially or even completely misunderstood by some of those who, many years after the event, took it on themselves to interpret him. It is my thesis that this is indeed what happened. That is why, if we are to discover anew the roots of the faith, we must ask some very basic questions. What do we know about Jesus? What was his message? What did he believe about himself? What is his significance for us today? It is to these issues that we now must turn.

THE STRANGER FROM GALILEE

NY SERIOUS person who tries to discover Jesus afresh has a formidable obstacle to overcome. Whether one is a devout churchgoer or not makes little difference. Most of us are simply loaded down with the accumulated baggage of half-truths, distortions, and plain, though well-meaning, falsehoods we have gleaned from Sunday-school days, sermons, and half-remembered Bible texts, as well as novels, plays, films, and newspapers. Along the way, traditional dogma about Jesus has become a part of the thinking of everyone in Western society—even those who have no vital faith at all. Somehow we have to try and jettison all of that, at least temporarily, and determine to come to our only real sources—the four Gospels—with minds as open as possible. No one can get rid of all of his or her preconceived ideas about such a complex subject, it's true. But if we want to catch a new vision, one that is relevant to us today, we have to make the effort.

Reading the New Testament to find out for ourselves what can be known about Jesus, we must first of all be surprised at the huge gaps in the information available. Despite what some popular preachers seem to imply, he remains in many ways a complete stranger. We know neither the precise date of his birth nor his exact age at the hour of his betrayal and crucifixion. We do not know what he looked like, whether he had a beard, the color of his hair or eyes. Admirers of the Shroud of Turin believe they have in that strange imprinted face the final answer to Jesus' appearance, and some artists have painted from it what they claim is a true portrait. Unfortunately, a number of experts are now convinced that the shroud is a pious forgery—forensic scientists in Chicago who specialize in art fraud say they have found traces of pigment on the linen. Until the Vatican (which has wisely refrained from declaring the shroud to be an authentic relic of Jesus) allows full Carbon-14 testing, we will have no reason to date it any earlier than the fourteenth century, the time of its first mention in any historical source. Even if research does show that it dates back to the first century A.D., this still would not prove that it was the shroud of Jesus himself, since the Romans crucified thousands of Jews during that period.

As for Jesus' early formative years, apart from the incident of going up to Jerusalem with his parents at the age of twelve, which is reported only in Luke's Gospel (2:41ff.)—when Joseph and Mary found him in the Temple listening to the scribes and asking them questions—we know nothing at all. We are not told whether he received any formal schooling, what he worked at, or whom he associated with. All the attention is focused on his ministry, death, and Resurrection, a timespan of from one and a half to three years depending on how you reconstruct the chronology. Thus it is impossible to compose a biography of Jesus in the modern sense of the word. The Gospel writers were not primarily historians or biographers—they were setting forth good news and writing from faith unto faith. Clearly, then, we need to be wary of those who would set forth the alleged psychology of Jesus or venture to tell us precisely what all his motives and intentions were. The detailed materials to base such statements on just aren't there.[1]

What We Do Know

Setting aside for a moment the complicated matter of the way the Gospels were composed and their general reliability, we can state with some measure of certainty the following: Jesus[2] was born a Jew, in Bethlehem, about six miles south of Jerusalem, and taken at an early age to Nazareth, a small town set on a hill in the Galilee, about one hundred miles north of the holy city. Some thirty years later he was baptized by John in the River Jordan. After a time spent meditating in the wilderness, he began to preach and heal the sick, casting "demons" out of many. He selected a dozen men—reminiscent of the twelve tribes of ancient Israel—as his disciples, commissioning them to preach the good news and heal as well. The poor, the sick, the outcasts, the oppressed, and the sinners were the chief objects of his loving concern. He taught both by word and by action; his speech was simple and rooted in the concrete realities of everyday living; he had a love of parables and earthy illustrations based on common necessities: yeast, salt, water, light.

At first his ministry, which was virtually confined to Jews and Jewish territory, was hailed with public enthusiasm. Some scholars believe that for a time even the Pharisees were seen as friends. But the storm-clouds of opposition soon began to gather. For a while Jesus kept moving from one rural hide-out to another as criticism by the religious establishment mounted. Finally, aware that the moment for final confrontation had come, he went to Jerusalem on the eve of Passover. After disappointing the crowds who hailed him with hosannas, hoping he would enter the holy city and proclaim himself the political Messiah who would liberate God's people from the yoke of Rome, he ate a special farewell meal with his followers. Then, as the religious and political powers plotted to rid themselves of this troublesome upstart, Judas, one of the Twelve, betrayed him by telling the authorities where they could take him captive without arousing the mob.

Judas may secretly have been a member of the Zealots (the Jewish party of revolt against Roman rule) who, having seen Jesus' seemingly miraculous powers, felt sure his Master both could and would show his hand and resort to heavenly violence (hordes of angels?) to usher in the Messianic Kingdom. The arrest in the garden, then, would serve as the goad to get Jesus to make his move. All this, of course, is speculation. Even the Gospel writers seem unsure of Judas' motives. (The verse in John 12:6 that declares he was a thief—he acted as treasurer for the group—is not supported by the first three Gospels and appears to represent a later attempt to vilify him.)

In any case, Jesus was taken into custody, flogged, mocked, and eventually hung on a cross where he died. Though the religious authorities accused him of blasphemy, he was put to death by the Romans, presumably for treason, on the grounds that as "King of the Jews" he represented a threat to public order. Significantly, when Pilate asked Jesus whether or not he thought he was a king, Jesus evaded the question by replying, "You say that I am a king," that is, "Those are your words, not mine" (John 18:37).[3]

Finally, though the women disciples had seen Jesus die—the others had all forsaken him and fled for their lives—on the third day some of these same women came running to tell Peter and the rest that they had seen Jesus alive once again. Soon the whole band were convinced that they too had met the Risen One, and they began to declare the news boldly in the streets. Where they had once been fearful and defeated, they now were ready to risk life itself for his sake. They were not yet called Christians—they were regarded as a fanatical Jewish sect—but the movement that was to be known as Christianity had begun.[4]

THE MESSAGE

Despite All Appearances, God Is in Control

TTEMPTING TO read the Gospels unshackled by the conventional wisdom or dogma of the past leads to some startling conclusions. Nowhere is this more obvious than when we ask the central question, What was Jesus' message? The various churches still operate on the axiom that his message concerned himself. Here, they say, is God-in-the-flesh, the Second Person of the Holy Trinity, walking about the Holy Land with a group of former fishermen, proclaiming himself as the only way of salvation. He is the content of his message; or rather, he is the message itself.

As I realized, however, the moment I could read the New Testament with any seriousness, and long before I had read a word of modern scholarly criticism, this is not what the Gospels say at all. If you begin with the Gospel According to St. Mark—the earliest of the four, written in about A.D. 64, approximately thirty years after the crucifixion[1]—you will find that Jesus came preaching the "good news of God" and saying: "The time is fulfilled and the Kingdom of God is at hand. Repent [have a change of heart] and put your trust in this good news" (1:14–15).

John's Gospel is quite different from the first three in tone and content and so will be considered at a later point. But if you take the combined witness of Mark, Matthew, and Luke,[2] it is obvious that Jesus came to proclaim what is translated as the Kingdom of God or of Heaven—the two are synonymous. His message had primarily to do not with himself but with God, whom he called Father. This message is a gospel (Greek *euangelion*) or good news because it makes the amazing affirmation that, despite all appearances to the contrary, God is in control of human affairs. Though it seems that evil or Satan rules the world and its empires—how else to account for the tragic history of Jesus' people, the Jews, their constant defeat by past enemies and their then-current oppression under the heel of Rome?—the very opposite is true. God has a Kingdom—in other words, He reigns supreme. This invisible reality has now drawn nigh, Jesus says, and can be experienced by even the most lowly or rejected. One day soon it will be revealed in all its might and glory.

Because the Kingdom of God is a spiritual reality (though it issues in concrete actions and must not be so spiritualized that it becomes restricted to some otherworldly sphere, far from that of human living) it is in a deep sense a mystery, or beyond the power of merely literal description. Thus Jesus uses a remarkably rich series of metaphors, similes, allegories, and parables to teach about it. His most characteristic mode of communication is analogy: "The Kingdom of God is like . . ." As you read the Gospels it quickly becomes clear that the idea of speaking in a literal or factual way about God, after the manner of many evangelists and preachers today, was totally foreign to Jesus. He, better than anyone else, knew that all language about the ultimate reality he called Father must of necessity be symbolic. That is why his chief vehicles for propounding the message he felt uniquely called to give were not creeds or dogmatic assertions but stories rooted in everyday experience. Most of the often horrific errors subsequently made in his name could have been avoided if his followers had taken this clue from their Master. It is the insistence on crude literalism and dogmatic orthodoxy where none is possible that has split the Christian Church into so many sects and denominations and that has so often made it the eager proponent of principles and causes Jesus never could have condoned.

The parables of the Kingdom bear out what the accounts of his temptation in the wilderness have already made clear (Mark 1:12 is expanded by both Matthew 4:12–17 and Luke 4:1–13). In meditating alone about his calling and ministry, Jesus rejects the use of miraculous caterings to the poor—the turning of stones to bread—and the seduction of temporal political power, with the danger of violence that inevitably implies. He has come to initiate a social revolution, the establishment of God's Kingdom on earth—the bringing in of a community of right-relatedness or righteousness for all humanity. He is convinced that this can only be accomplished by peaceful means, a revolution of the heart and will. Its beginnings are small and unimpressive—like a grain of mustard seed, or the yeast hidden in a lump of dough. But eventually it will grow and spread until it fills the entire world. We are meant to seek it above all else, like a pearl of great price; we enter it with simple trust, like a little child. This Kingdom is based on peace—not the peace of a pietistic, "safe in the arms of Jesus" retreat from this world, but the kind designated by the Hebrew word *shalom:* a social peace whose basic ingredient is justice for all, particularly those at the bottom of the heap. This Kingdom takes its inspiration from the living God, but it is rooted firmly in this world. The coming of the Kingdom is God's will being done "on earth, as it is in heaven."

Significantly, those who enter the Kingdom, according to Jesus, are not the obviously, ostentatiously religious. He reserves his harshest condemnations for the scribes, Pharisees, and Sadducees—the professional holy men of the time. Harlots, tax gatherers, and all kinds of other "sinners" are accepted first because of their deep awareness of their need, their eagerness to receive God's gift of right-relatedness to Him, to themselves, and to their fellows, and their lack of illusions about their own merits or status. As a physician, Jesus has come to heal those who realize their sickness. The publican who stands in the temple with his head downcast, praying, "God be merciful to me, a sinner" has the righteousness of the Kingdom; the Pharisee, proud of his religiosity, is rejected.

To Save from Fear

Traditional Christian teaching holds that Jesus' mission was to save us from our sins—to "take away the sins of the world." But if you read the Gospels with an open mind, you will discover that this orthodox contention is not borne out. His proclamation of the good news about the Kingdom was accompanied by a summons to repent, that is, to have a radical change of heart, mind, and will. Yes, this does imply that there is something essentially wrong with us as human beings. We need a physician; we need salvation—that is, healing or wholeness. But as we read on we see that it is neither sin in general nor specific sins that constitute the problem. Jesus' attitude to sin is that it already has a remedy—it can be and indeed is forgiven. As John Macmurray once put it: "This is, perhaps, the most revolutionary of his teachings. He proposes to deal with sin by forgiving it, instead of by punishing it."[3] He taught that we too have a right to forgive sins and that there should be no limits to our use of that right.

If we look carefully, we find that it is not the disciples' sins that Jesus takes issue with; it is their lack of faith. He is constantly reported as chiding them for their fearfulness and anxiety: "How is that ye have no faith?" "Why are ye so full of fear?" Repeatedly he urges them to take courage, to be confident, to trust (see, for example, Matthew 8:26, Mark 4:40, Luke 12:32). What is really significant in Jesus' frequent juxtaposition of faith and fear is that for the most part the word "faith" has no specific object—there is no question of faith in creeds, dogmas, or other propositional truths. He uses "faith" or "confidence" in a general sense to describe a basic emotional and mental outlook. Similarly, the fear Jesus talks about is without specific object. He sees the central human problem or illness as a fearful, distrusting state of mind—an anxious, defensive attitude and approach to life itself. When we are afraid, we act like the steward in the parable who said, "I was afraid and so I hid my talent in the earth"; he was metaphorically "cast into the outer darkness." It is this same fear—projected on a global scale—that has presented us today with the nuclear nightmare. Fear leads to a mania for "security" and, in the process, ever greater insecurity for all.

Jesus knew that ultimately life comes down to personal relations, to community and friendship (see John 15:12–15). But these depend on trust, and their greatest enemy is fear. Macmurray develops this theme: fear, he says, "tends to create what we are afraid of. Any intimate relation with another person depends on mutual trust. If I fear to lose the relationship, I have already diminished the trust. If I go on the defensive for fear of losing my friend; if I do something to prevent what I fear then I poison the relationship and make its loss more likely."[4] Fearful persons tend to retreat from life, from others, from themselves. Their lives become stilted, lacking in spontaneity or energy. They become less than themselves, less than they were always intended to be. By contrast, when we begin to trust, to relax in the knowledge that this is God's world and in His hands—that is, as we enter into the Kingdom—life begins to flow. We are no longer on the lookout for danger but open, accepting of others, uninhibited. Constraint is gone and life, instead of threatening, begins to sparkle with opportunity. As Jesus put it, vividly: "Out of [one's] innermost being shall flow rivers of living water" (John 7:38).

Thus we can define the intention or mission of Jesus as one of liberating people from their fear and re-establishing the faith and trust that allow life to flow. But if we agree in this diagnosis of the central human problem (corroborated in our time by such psychoanalysts as Carl Jung) the question is, How can it be remedied? It is not enough simply to tell people not to be afraid, or urge them to keep a stiff upper lip. Jesus' own sense of trust in life undoubtedly came from his intimate sense of God's presence and power or kingship over all things. So in a deep sense his command to have faith is theologically based—on the vision of God that he held and that he revealed in his own life and teaching.

But there is more. If his first commandment was to have faith, his second was to "love one another." In fact, love is Jesus' antidote to fear; he was committed to what Henry Drummond called the "expulsive power of a new emotion."[5] He tells his followers to love one another "as I have loved you." Later in the New Testament we learn that "perfect love casts out fear" (I John 4:18). Who has perfect love? None of us would dare make the claim. But the disciples saw that love in action in Jesus' life and, particularly, in his manner of dying. And, down the ages, it has retained its healing power. The perfect love and forgiveness shown by Jesus give us a glimpse into the inner nature of the very ground of our existence, and recognition of this fact awakens a response of love in return: "We love him because he first loved us" (I John 4:19). It is this love that not only expells fear, but goes out in reconciling power into the whole of society. It loves its neighbor as itself. Any church built on these principles has, in the end, to exist not for itself or its own members, but for the world.

THE MYTH OF THE VIRGIN BIRTH

I N THE summer of 1984 there was a major theological row in Britain over the consecration of Rev. David Jenkins as Bishop of Durham, the fourth most important See in the Church of England (after Canterbury, York, and London). During the ceremony protesters paraded outside the cathedral and inside one man shouted aloud, "This is a blasphemy against Christ!"

The reason for the furore was Jenkins's well-known scepticism on some key points of orthodox belief. The former professor of theology at Leeds University had openly stated his doubts about the Virgin Birth, the miracles, and the Resurrection of Jesus, saying that these events may well not have happened as described in the Bible. A subsequent poll of England's thirty-nine bishops revealed he was not alone. About a third of them reported that they share his scepticism. Over twelve thousand Anglicans, chiefly from the two extremes— the High Church party and the Evangelicals—signed a petition of protest, but the Archbishop who presided at the consecration told them and members of the media that he was quite satisfied with Jenkins's faith. York Minster was the site of the service, and when, shortly afterwards, the great cathedral nearly burned to the ground, there were many who said the fire was an obvious sign of God's displeasure.

The truth is that the bishop and those who agreed with him have some fairly weighty evidence on their side, at least where the Virgin Birth is concerned. The great Apostle St. Paul nowhere mentions this "miracle," nor does the earliest Gospel, that of Mark; the fourth Gospel, John's, has no birth narrative at all. The story belongs uniquely to Luke and Matthew, and even they do not always agree.[1] In fact, the more you read the two Gospels concerned, the more you become aware that the birth legends are pious embroidery on the main story. Having come to believe in Jesus, after the events of the Resurrection, as God Incarnate, the Gospel writers had a natural impulse to seek grounds for a fittingly supernatural conception, and to find them they looked to the only Bible they had: the Old Testament. We know from the Apostolic sermons reported in Acts that the Twelve spent much of their time and energy reading and reinterpreting the Old Testament.[2] They were quick to spot verses and prophecies that could be applied to Jesus, even if it meant taking them out of their original contexts and in some cases even twisting them.

Isaiah 7:14 is an example. In the context of a prophecy for King Ahaz, who fears an alliance of Syria and Ephraim against him, the verse reads: "Therefore the Lord himself shall give you a sign; behold, a young woman shall conceive and bear a son, and shall call his name Immanuel." The name Immanuel means "God is with us." What has to be stressed is that in taking this verse to refer to Jesus, as Matthew does (2:23), the early Church did not use the original Hebrew text, which speaks of a young woman of marriageable age ('almah), but instead relied on the Greek translation known as the Septuagint. In Greek the word used was *parthenos,* which can mean a virgin.

Isaiah is not talking about a virgin—for which there was a perfectly good Hebrew word (*bethulah*)—but about a young woman who may or may not already be married. Thus most good modern translations say simply "a young woman." There is no reference whatever to the birth of Jesus more than seven hundred years later. The context shows without question that the prophecy is to be fulfilled—the child is to be born—in the immediate future, because this "sign" is intended as a response to a pressing emergency. The king's lack of trust in the Lord is to be rebuked by the child's name, "God is with us." The exact identity of either the child or the mother is of little import to the prophet; what matters is the name itself and the way it expresses the mother's faith. Nevertheless, lifted out of its setting, mistranslated, and placed in Matthew's account of Jesus' birth, the verse has played a key role in the making of the myth.

For a complete analysis of the mythical nature of the entire cycle of infancy narratives in Luke and Matthew, I refer readers to the latest and most comprehensive commentary on Matthew by the late Rev. F. W. Beare, professor emeritus of Trinity College, Toronto, from which I quote the following: "The Matthean infancy narratives are variations on ancient themes of myth and legend which recur widely in the Near and Middle East. The discovery of the child, and his miraculous escape from the enemies who threaten his life—these are primary motifs of the stories in themselves; and they are crossed by the theological preoccupation of the evangelist—the fulfilment of prophecy, the rejection of the Saviour by the rulers of Israel and his acknowledgement by strangers to the covenants of promise, harbingers of the Gentiles who will be gathered into the church that is to be. . . . There is no point in debating the historicity of such a chain of stories; whatever significance they possess does not lie in any possible kernel of historical fact which may be embedded in them, but in the purpose which they are intended to serve as they are understood by Matthew."[3]

Regarding the story of the mysterious star—about which volumes of very silly speculation have been written by those with more credulity than common sense—Beare rightly points out that a comet or any kind of star would never be of use in guiding people from Jerusalem to Bethlehem, a distance of about six miles; nor would it "come to rest" over one particular house. The concept of a new star coming into the heavens to signal the birth of a great man, is, as Beare also notes, almost a routine feature of Hellenistic legends of that time. The theme of threats to the child's life is also extremely ancient. Beare reminds us that in the great Osiris myth, the life of the child Horus is threatened by Set. "And in Babylonia the infant Sargon is miraculously preserved from the murderous assaults of his enemies. All you have to do is to re-read the story of the Exodus to see the parallels in Moses' life. For Matthew, Jesus is a Second Moses—and more."[4]

It is significant that about A.D. 250 Origen (185–254), one of the earliest great Christian scholars, answered attacks against the idea of the Virgin Birth by citing similar events in pagan stories of deities or semi-deities. In his *Contra Celsum* he bluntly says that when speaking to Greeks it is quite in order to quote Greek myths, "lest we appear to be the only people to have related this incredible story." He then goes on to tell how when Plato was born, Ariston was hindered from having sexual intercourse with his mother until she had given birth to the child she had by the god Apollo.[5] Origen's quarrel with Celsus (a pagan critic of Christianity who lived some seventy years earlier) gives ample evidence that in those days anyone regarded as in any way extraordinary could be called "divine" and be the subject of stories not only of miraculous birth, but of healing miracles, deification, and, ultimately, appearances after death.

For me, however, what clinches the conviction that the Virgin Birth is pure myth is the Gospel evidence that Mary herself had no inkling of her son's true identity. If you leave the infancy stories on one side and look at the rest of the Gospels, Mary's lack of awareness is astonishing. Women do not have babies without either intercourse or a form of artificial insemination. If she had indeed conceived miraculously she would have known it and would have had at least some insight into the allegedly unique nature of her son. She shows none. Indeed, at one point early in Jesus' ministry, Mary and some close relatives actually come to apprehend him and take him home because they think him to be insane (Mark 3:21). "When they heard that he was there, his family members came with the express purpose of taking charge of him. Their reason, they said, was that he was 'beside himself.'"[6] The Magnificat and other sections from the opening chapters of Matthew and Luke cannot be used as proof that Mary knew, since it is their historicity itself that is in question.

Modern knowledge of reproduction and genetics, of course, also rules out a virgin birth. We know it takes the genetic material—with all its history—from two parents to create a new person. The orthodox doctrine requires that Jesus have no normal genetic traits of any male forbears whatever. In fact, if parthenogenesis (virgin birth) were to occur, only a female baby could result, since there would be no Y chromosome from a male sperm.

The story of how the cult of Mary grew from its flimsy origins to a full-fledged Mariolatry by the end of the fourth century is a fascinating study in the growth of a myth.[7] By the time of St. Augustine (A.D. 354–430) prayers were being addressed to her and it was widely believed that her own birth had been miraculous; that her womb was in no way changed by having given birth (Augustine argued that if Christ could go through closed doors after his Resurrection, there was no reason he could not leave her womb without violating it in any way); and that she remained perpetually without sin. Earlier, however, some of the scholars held different opinions. For example, Tertullian (*ca.* 160–230) opposed Irenaeus and Clement of Alexandria in their doctrine that Mary's childbearing was free from normal physical travail or birth pangs. He also insisted that she went on to have normal sexual relations with Joseph after the birth of Jesus, although Origen (who later emasculated himself to escape the risk of sexual sin) argued that she remained a virgin *post partum* and for the rest of her life; he took the references to Jesus' "brethren" in the Greek text of the New Testament to refer to half-brothers belonging to Joseph but not to Mary. The polemics over such topics as Mary's sinlessness and moral perfection were lengthy and intricate. At any rate, by the mid-fifth century, when the debates over the question of explaining Christ's divinity-humanity were at their peak, Mary was already beginning to be called Theotokos, Mother of God. That some were treating her as a goddess can be inferred from the remark of Nestorius (died *ca.* 451) that he did not mind people's calling her Mother of God as long as they stopped short of full worship, "as if she were a goddess."[8]

The orthodox title Theotokos, Mother of God, is in my view a blasphemy against the Almighty—one from which Jesus himself would have recoiled, as would any pious Jew. As a matter of fact, according to the Gospels, Jesus' own treatment of Mary, while respectful, was at times quite sharp. For examples, see the story of the changing of water into wine (John 2:1ff.)—when Mary tells him they have run out of wine, Jesus replies, "Woman, what have I to do with thee?"—and the passages in the Synoptics where Jesus is told his mother and brothers are outside asking for him and he responds with the question, "Who is my mother and my brethren?"; he then goes on to say his real family consists of all those who do the will of God, the heavenly Father. There is not one iota of evidence in the text that Jesus attributed *any* kind of special status to his mother. True, in John he tells the "beloved disciple" to take Mary home from the cross and treat her as his own mother, but that hardly seems more than any thoughtful son would request.

There are several important factors at work, then, in the dogma of the Virgin Birth. There is the attempt by the evangelists to provide a fitting theological underpinning for their belief in the exalted nature of Jesus. There is also a deep antisexual bias, a feeling that sexual intercourse itself is evil (even though Genesis plainly teaches the goodness of the whole created order). This bias can be seen most blatantly in the way the churches—most notably the Eastern Orthodox and the Roman Catholic—have on the one hand praised Mary as an example to all women of chastity and pure womanhood while on the other hand stripping her of every vestige of true female sexuality. In such a theology there are really only virgins and whores, with no room for anything in between. At the same time the evolution of Mariolatry, based on a literal belief in the Virgin Birth, has been evidence of an attempt—subconscious or even unconscious—to supply a lack of the feminine principle in the doctrine of God. As the great psychotherapist Carl Jung noted in his critique of orthodox Christianity, the cult of Mary fills a deeply felt psychological need, especially among a celibate priesthood, for the feminine aspect he called the anima (even so, Jung believed that the doctrine of the Trinity was unduly male-oriented). Nevertheless, supporting a mythology that can play a beneficial role in the psyche does not mean one must fail to acknowledge its non-historical foundations.[9]

THE HUMANITY OF JESUS

WHATEVER ELSE one may believe about Jesus, it is clear both from the New Testament documents and from the creeds of the early Church that he was a fully human being. He knew hunger, thirst, and weariness; he endured pain, grief, and the agony of doubt; he experienced birth and death. His appearance must have been ordinary, for on several occasions when trouble was brewing he was able simply to lose himself in the crowds. The Church of the first few centuries had little trouble selling the idea of God-in-human-form to a non-Jewish audience: this kind of myth was commonplace at the time. The real difficulty lay in convincing people that his humanity was real, that God could really suffer and die. The intellectual obstacle was overcome for many in the heresy known as Docetism, from the Greek *dokein*, to seem. The argument took the line that although Jesus appeared to be human, this was merely an illusion. He was in fact God disguised as a man. (I have described this syndrome elsewhere as the Superman-Clark Kent mode of thought: Jesus as the celestial visitor who comes from outer space, lives on earth disguised as one of us, and then goes back to his glorious home in the skies.)

Today theologians say the main obstruction to faith is not so much Jesus' humanity as his divinity. That may be so, but closer examination reveals that Docetism is very much alive and well in Christian circles. The churches say the right things about his being fully human, but they refuse to follow the logic of their contentions: the Jesus they preach is an unearthly figure very far removed from what most of us think of as human. He remains a God-in-disguise, one who during his days on earth was the embodiment of intellectual and moral perfection, knowing none of the limitations that beset normal mortals. His humanity has been sacrificed on the altar of deity.

The churches' real attitude can easily be discovered by asking some questions about Jesus' sexuality. The Roman Catholic Church and those Anglicans opposed to women's ordination to the priesthood make much of the fact that Jesus was male. But that is where they drop the matter. Embarrassed dismay is the first reaction from clergy and laity alike when anyone dares discuss the possibility that Jesus was married. Most probably he was not, but the idea ought not to offend as it does. One or two theologians have had the temerity to point out that if Jesus' humanity is to be taken with any seriousness one must be prepared to say that he knew sexual desire, that as a male he probably experienced nocturnal erections, and that the moment when Mary Magdalene dried his feet with her hair could well have been erotically charged. These suggestions have occasioned deep shock among the faithful. Why should they? Here, as in the traditional view of his mother Mary as "perpetual virgin," the true depths of human sexuality have been stripped away, leaving only a shadow of any real, flesh-and-blood humanity. It is one thing to argue that since the Bible gives no evidence of any sexual activity on the part of Jesus, he was "without sin" in this area of life; it is something quite different to deny that he experienced the normal sexual stirrings and feelings that are a rudimentary element of what it is to be human. The letter to the Hebrews indicates in several places that Jesus was tempted in all the ways we ourselves are tempted (2:16–18); it also states he had to "learn obedience" to God through the various experiences he suffered (5:8).

Even more dismaying to many than the subject of Jesus' sexual feelings is the idea that he could have shared in any of the limitations to which all human beings are prone—that he may have been biased or prejudiced on certain topics, ignorant on others, and subject to the mistakes that are part of any truly human development. Because official doctrine, despite all disclaimers, is really about a God-in-disguise, the earthly Jesus is habitually seen as a being perfect in every way, morally and intellectually. He only seems to be a man; really he is a superman with all the perfection and power of God Himself. Yet surely this an after-the-fact reading back into Jesus' life of the dogmas of a later age.

The doctrine of a sinless paragon who never erred in any

fashion has caused enormous psychological harm to those who have believed that being a Christian means being "another Jesus." This over-scrupulous ambition entails a perfectionism and an inability to accept cheerfully one's own humanity that together compose a major source of depression and even breakdown among clergy and faithful alike. It is actually a spiritual axiom that if as a believer you do not take Jesus' humanity with full honesty and seriousness, you will find it well-nigh impossible to accept your own. What is interesting is the fact that although the New Testament authors were writing from the perspective of faith and in order to promote faith in a Risen Lord—a faith that colored all their work—their accounts nevertheless show stages of growth, a gradual maturing of Jesus' thinking.

Luke's Gospel alone gives us any account of Jesus between his birth and the baptism by John just before he began his ministry. In Luke 2:41ff. we are told of a visit with his parents to the Temple at Jerusalem when he was twelve years old. Most people who are vaguely familiar with this passage assume that when Jesus stayed behind in the Temple—his parents had left, assuming he was with their group from Nazareth and then had to come back to the city looking for him— he was instructing the professors there. According to the text, however, he was doing nothing of the sort. It says he was listening to the teachers and asking them questions—that is, he was in a learning situation. Luke ends the passage by saying Jesus went on progressing in wisdom and stature "and found favor with both God and men" (2:52; compare 2:40).

During the ministry itself, there were a number of occasions when Jesus either lost his temper or made it very plain he was angry. The most obvious examples are the cursing of the barren fig tree and the cleansing of the Temple. The story of the fig tree is very strange. Luke omits it altogether, while Mark tries to soften the incident with a few words about forgiveness. He tells us that while Jesus and his disciples were walking from Bethany—the small village just east of Jerusalem where his friends Lazarus, Martha, and Mary lived—Jesus felt hungry. Seeing a fig tree covered with leaves at the side of the road, he went over to see if it had any fruit. He found none, "because it was not the right season for figs."

Jesus then cursed the tree: "May you never bear fruit again!" When they passed by the same place a day or so later, the tree had withered up. Peter, remembering the incident, said to Jesus, "Rabbi, look how the fig tree which you cursed has dried up." Jesus then told him to have faith in God because faith can "move mountains." Alarmed, perhaps, at the possibility that his readers might use this passage to justify cursing their enemies, Mark has Jesus add an admonition: "When you stand, praying, if you have any grudge against anyone, forgive them so that your heavenly father may forgive your sins" (11:12–25).

Attempts to spiritualize or allegorize this passage have not been successful. It does not read like an acted parable, the scholars point out. They speculate that the story grew around some saying of Jesus in the vicinity of a conspicuous dead tree near Jerusalem, or that it is a translation of the parable of the barren fig tree (Luke 13:6ff.) into actual incident. Neither answer is very satisfactory, and unless we are prepared to ignore it completely, we are forced to admit that the story has at its core an occasion on which Jesus gave way to petulance and vindictive wrath.

Another instance of anger is the cleansing of the Temple, which the first three Gospels set just before the trial and crucifixion, but John puts at the very outset of the public ministry. Here the anger is righteous, but it is anger all the same, and violent at that. We are told Jesus entered the outer court of the Temple and poured the money-changers' coins on the floor as he threw their tables over. The energy and rage described, as well as the symbolic nature of the action, suggest an Old Testament prophet filled with zeal for the House of the Lord. The incident did have a spiritual meaning; but it was the act of a real human being nonetheless, one with which we can readily identify.

Most of Jesus' ministry took place in the northern district of Israel, the Galilee, and it is clear he thought of his mission as directed to the Jews, not to the world at large. On one occasion, though, we find him entering Gentile territory—not to evangelize but to lie low; he wanted to avoid Herod and the Pharisees while having some time alone with the twelve disciples to train them. Mark tells us (7:24ff.) that he went into the region of Tyre and found lodging in a certain house. He did not want his whereabouts known, but "it was impossible for him to escape attention." A Greek woman, of Syrophoenician origin, had a daughter "sick with an unclean spirit." Hearing Jesus was in the neighborhood, she came and, falling at his feet in supplication, asked him to "cast out the demons" from the little girl. Jesus' reply is noteworthy. He rebuked her: "Let the children be fed first, for it is not right to take the children's bread and cast it to the household dogs." She replied, "Sir, even the dogs eat the scraps under the children's table." She understood that Jesus was putting her off by saying his teaching was first and foremost for his own people. Her quick-witted response, however, changed his mind. His reply was this: "Because of your answer, go. The demon has departed from your daughter." She went home to find her daughter healed.

Luke does not include this story, but Matthew gives an even fuller account (15:21ff.). He says the woman had become a nuisance by following the disciples and their Master, crying for help, and that Jesus began by ignoring her. When the Twelve asked him to do something for her, Jesus explicitly stated, "I am not sent to any except to the lost sheep of the House of Israel." But after speaking with her he said: "O woman, your faith is very great. You may have what you desire." I agree with those who argue that this awkward and unflattering passage would never have been reported if it had not been rooted in a real event, and who see it as an example of racial prejudice on Jesus' part. Only when his prejudice is challenged by the foreigner's intelligence and/or faith is he forced to revise both his opinion and his course of action. There is no other way to take the passage that makes sense and does justice to its surprising language. The woman's words opened a new horizon in his thinking. He had learned a new tolerance.[1]

Finally, to hear many Christians—including clergy—talk, you would think the man Jesus possessed the omniscience usually attributed to God—that his knowledge was infinite and he could not make a mistake. But this again is to make nonsense of his humanity. If Jesus was, as the Bible and the creeds insist, "very man of very man," it follows that he shared the information, views, and knowledge of his time. This is not to say he uncritically accepted all the popular wisdom of his day; plainly he did not. In terms of spiritual insight he was far beyond his contemporaries, his predecessors, and those who would follow him. But it would be folly to suppose he did not share, for instance, the belief that the earth was the center of the universe, or that some human ailments were caused by demons. On matters of science, as on many others, he remained very much part of the culture in which he lived. In other words, he had specifically human limitations; he was "conditioned" by his cultural environment.

Jesus made no claims to infallibility. He himself expressed ignorance over the precise moment of the Second Coming or end of this world order: "But concerning that day or hour nobody knows, not the angels, nor the son, but the Father alone" (Mark 13:32). Nevertheless, he apparently expected the cataclysmic event to occur very soon—in fact, during the lifetime of some of his followers—for two verses earlier he states, "Truly I say to you that this generation will not pass away before all these things come to pass."

Matthew has Jesus put the matter much more urgently. He tells the disciples that they will not have preached in all the cities of Israel on their mission tour "before the Son of man be come" to usher in the end-time (10:23). The same erroneous opinion was firmly held by the early Church; indeed, one of St. Paul's earliest letters reprimands a group of Christians who are so sure of an imminent end that they have stopped working for a living. A similar kind of apocalyptic expectation and fervor has recurred regularly throughout the history of the Church, especially at pivotal moments of the collapse of empires or other periods of rapid social change. Thus it is not surprising that today it figures prominently in the appeal of many of the newer sects in the United States and elsewhere and is at the very heart of the newly vigorous and outspoken fundamentalist movement. You can laugh, perhaps, when you see a bumper sticker which informs other drivers that in the event of the "Rapture" the car in question will be left without its occupants. But for many this is no joke. They expect to be "raptured" to heaven when the nuclear missiles start to demolish planet Earth.

For Jesus to be fully human he had to be capable of error. Traditionally he has too often been portrayed as remote, austere, and condemning; he has been made so perfect in every way as to have little connection with real human beings. His humanity has been lost, swallowed up by an impossible ideal.

THE TEACHINGS OF JESUS

On Sex

I FIND it very odd that the churches—particularly the Roman Catholic Church and the most orthodox Protestant groups—have always seemed almost obsessed with sex and sexual matters when Jesus himself had so little to say on the topic. He has left us no specific wisdom on such matters as abortion, contraception, artificial insemination, or even premarital sex. Yet some Church leaders give the impression he spoke of little else.

In Chapter 10 of Mark's Gospel Jesus is tested on the subject of divorce by the Pharisees, who ask him whether he agrees with Moses' rulings (see Deuteronomy 24). Jesus goes back beyond what Deuteronomy says to Genesis (also believed by him and his contemporaries to have been written by Moses). Here first of all is the Deuteronomy passage on which the divorce practices of Jesus' day were based: "When a man hath taken a wife, and married her, and it come to pass that she find no favour in his eyes . . . then let him write her a bill of divorcement, and give it in her hand, and send her out of his house. And when she is departed out of his house she may go and be another man's wife" (Deut. 24:1–2, KJV).

Here is the passage in Mark: "And the Pharisees came to him, and asked him, Is it lawful for a man to put away his wife? tempting him. And he answered . . . What did Moses command you? And they said, he suffered to write a bill of divorcement and to put her away. Jesus answered, For the hardness of your heart he wrote you this precept. But from the beginning of the creation God made them male and female. For this cause shall a man leave his father and mother, and cleave to his wife. And they twain shall be one flesh. What God hath joined together, let no man put asunder" (Mark 10:2–9, KJV).

When the disciples question him privately about this teaching, Jesus elaborates, saying that for either party (in Judaism only the man had this right) to divorce the other means forcing the divorced spouse to commit adultery if he or she later marries someone else. At first sight, it seems Jesus is taking a very rigorous stance, correcting one of Moses' sayings with another and affirming the absolute indissolubility of marriage. Some churches, most notably the Roman Catholic, have based their ban on remarriage after divorce on this interpretation. In fact, most commentators believe that he is not here considering the issue of whether or not adultery justifies divorce; rather, he is going to the heart of the divine order willed by God and saying that the spiritual ideal is that of a lifetime commitment; ideally, marriage is indissoluble. It is significant that Matthew's version of the same incident contains an "escape clause": "And whosoever shall put away his wife except it be for fornication [adultery] and shall marry another . . ." (19:9, KJV); in other words, Matthew feared that the saying in Mark could be misunderstood, and so clarified the meaning by making adultery the exception to the apparent prohibition of divorce. If he rightly interpreted what Jesus had in mind, we can say that Jesus allowed room for human error. Marriage may be indissoluble ideally, but if adultery can lead to divorce, the indissolubility is not an absolute. Absolutes by definition admit of no exceptions.

I believe this interpretation throws light on another strand of Jesus' teaching about sexual matters. In the Sermon on the Mount, he insists that the Pharisees' pride in keeping the Ten Commandments is misplaced. He stresses that sin is not so much a matter of externals as an affair of the heart or the inner self. True virtue, he explains, is much more than not actually committing murder or adultery; to be angry with one's brother "without cause" is to have contemplated murder; to look at a woman "to lust after her" means one has already committed adultery with her "in his heart" (Matt. 5:20ff., KJV). Thus he says: "Except your righteousness shall exceed the righteousness of the scribes and Pharisees, ye shall in no case enter into the kingdom of heaven." Similarly in Mark, during a discussion of whether or not it was important to observe the ritual washings of traditional Judaism, Jesus once again radicalizes ethics by saying it is not what happens outside a person that matters: "There is nothing from without a person that entering into him can defile him: but those things which come out of him, those are the things which defile him" (7:15). In his explanation to the disciples in private, he points out that it is from the heart that all evils, including adulteries or sexual sins (Greek *porneiai*), proceed.

We have to see Jesus' views on sexual sin in the context of his situation. He was being attacked by the rigidly minded religious elite for spending time with outright sinners and for not observing the taboos and rules of external religion. His point is that their alleged holiness is really a sham because they spend so much time and effort keeping up appearances that they are unaware of the "sin" in their hearts. Harlots and other sinners go into the Kingdom ahead of the self-righteous because they at least *know* their true spiritual state and are not guilty of the greatest sin of all—pride. Because they have no illusions about their worthiness, they are in a position to accept God's free forgiveness. Jesus was not trying to hold up an impossible ideal. He was as aware as anyone could be that normal human beings have angry thoughts from time to time and that sexual fantasies come unbidden to most people. His point is that if you really care about sexual purity, say, you must begin by examining your own thoughts, not by taking pride and condemning others simply because you have never committed adultery by some external act.

Jesus' attitude towards those who had committed sexual sins was one of compassion and understanding. This is shown clearly in his willingness to associate with people publicly known to be sexually delinquent—he would never have been accused of being friendly with prostitutes and others unless there was a sound basis for the charge, nor would the Gospel writers have included such potentially damaging information. The passage about the woman caught in the act of adultery (John 8) is agreed by scholars to belong not to the original Gospel of John, but to one of the Synoptic Gospels, possibly Luke. In any case, it is a key indication of Jesus' attitude to sexual offences. He tells her that he does not condemn her—because he realizes God does not condemn her—and then adds: "Go and sin no more" (8:1–11).

Since this is really all Jesus had to say specifically about sex—compared with pronouncement after pronouncement about the sin of pride and hypocrisy on the part of the religious establishment—it is fairly easy to summarize. First, he saw sexual misdemeanors such as adultery as no more and no less evil than other sins. Note, for example, how in the Mark passage already cited (7:1ff.) he is reported to have listed adulteries together with covetousness, pride, foolishness, and blasphemy ("All these evils come from within and defile . . ."). Second, the remedy for errors in this realm is the same as that for other sins—that is, acknowledgment of failure, acceptance of forgiveness, and a firm intent to "go and sin no more." We can safely say that he laid down no detailed code of sexual conduct. As noted above, there are no rules for the unmarried, the engaged, the widowed, the homosexual, the couple facing an unwanted pregnancy, the infertile couple wondering about artificial insemination. This does not mean, however, that his would-be followers can do whatever they like sexually and still be faithful to his teachings. All conduct has to be judged by the two over-arching principles or commandments (the only two he gave): love of God and love of neighbor "as thyself." These guidelines are certainly much less explicit and directive than those who want to avoid thinking for themselves or bearing the stress of ambiguity would like to see; anyone searching for simple, black-and-white solutions here is doomed to disappointment.

On Prayer

"Early in the morning, while it was still dark, he arose and going out of the house to a solitary place he spent time in prayer" (Mark 1:35).

All of the Gospels witness to the fact that earnest prayer was a central feature of Jesus' own spiritual life. There is no point at which we sense his full humanity, his essential oneness with ourselves, more powerfully than when we see and hear him praying to his Father. In fact, unless we are prepared to believe that his prayer-dependence on God was nothing more than a sham for our edification, a mere act to set us a good example, it is impossible to cling to the orthodox teaching that Jesus was really God Himself walking about in human form, the Second Person of the Trinity. The concept of God praying—let alone praying to Himself—is incomprehensible to me. To say that it was simply the human side of Jesus talking to God the Father (rather than to his own divine nature as Son of God) is to posit a kind of schizophrenia that is incompatible with any belief in Jesus' full humanity.

Nor does Jesus anywhere tell either his disciples or the crowd in general to pray to him. Prayer is to be addressed to God the heavenly Father always. Thus the habit of many Christians of addressing prayers to Jesus has scant support. He does talk about praying "in my name," but that is a different matter altogether.[1] To pray "in his name" means to pray according to the vision of God one has come to know in him. Thus prayer in Jesus' name is prayer offered according to the character and teaching of Jesus. Clearly, this perspective rules out any magical use of prayer for one's own material gain (or for winning at professional sports). That said, let us see what the Gospels can tell us about Jesus' own attitude to prayer.

In Mark 9:17ff. we have the story of a boy possessed by a "deaf and dumb spirit." When the disciples try to heal him they fail, but Jesus casts out the spirit. The disciples then ask him why they were impotent to do it. He replies, "This kind can come forth by nothing except by prayer and fasting" (v. 29). Some commentators believe this is an addition to the text by the early Church, which may have found prayer and fasting necessary before exorcisms. But if it is an authentic saying of Jesus, it is further evidence of his own felt need for constant prayer in his war against evil and disease.

Mark does not include what has come to be known as the Lord's Prayer. His longest section dealing with Jesus' views on prayer comes in the context of the cursing of the fig tree. Here is what Jesus says about prayer: "Have faith [confidence or trust] in God. Truly I tell you, whoever says to this mountain, be moved hence and thrown into the sea and does not doubt in his heart but has faith that what he says is coming to pass, it will be so for him. Therefore I tell you, whatsoever you pray and ask for, believe that you have received, and it will be so for you. And whenever you stand praying, forgive anyone against whom you have complaint so that your Father in heaven may forgive you your trespasses" (11:21ff.).

Here, as nearly always, Jesus is speaking spiritually. The mountain is a metaphor, not meant to be taken literally. Nor is the passage confirmation of the absurd notion that prayer is some kind of spiritual blank cheque, a way of extorting from God gifts He would not otherwise give or favors denied to the rest of humankind. He is saying that those who have an attitude of expectant faith as they seek to grow spiritually are already receiving what they ask for; spiritual "mountains" can be brought low.

At the Last Supper, the next reference to prayer in Mark, we find Jesus giving the traditional blessing or prayer of thanks over the bread and the cup, following precisely the pattern that the head of any Jewish family at the time would have used. Beginning "Blessed be thou, Lord God . . .", it is a simple grace or giving of praise to the Almighty Creator.

This incident is followed closely by the prayer of agony in the garden of Gethsemane: "If it be possible, let this hour pass from me." Here Jesus is pleading with God as would any pious person about to face death; there is no sense of his being a divinity who is in full charge and knows he is to be delivered. He has absolute trust and faith in God that somehow there will be a triumph, but all is really in the hands of the Father. The idea that this is God talking to Himself, however you divide up the Persons, makes no sense whatever. He repeats his prayer three times, addressing God as "Abba" (the Aramaic word of affection or intimacy, akin to our "daddy" or "papa"); "Abba, Father, all things are possible unto thee; take away this cup from me: nevertheless, not what I will, but what thou wilt" (14:36, KJV). Undoubtedly these words of human grief and deep desire to avoid death are genuine. No adulator or propagandist out to portray a God-in-human-form would ever have invented such an episode. The words show intense intimacy and filial dependence; there is radical trust, but also very human doubt and fear. This is not some mythical divinity acting a part, but a real human being, with all the weaknesses flesh is prone to.

The truth of Jesus' humanity is seen most vividly and poignantly when we come to the last prayer recorded in Mark. As he hangs in agony on the cross, mocked by his tormentors and aware, as they are, of the traditional Jewish view that anyone who "hangs upon a tree" is cursed by God, he cries out the terrible, haunting "*Eloi, Eloi, lama sabachthani?*": "My

God, my God, why have you forsaken me?" These are the very words that begin Psalm 22: "My God, my God, why hast thou forsaken me? Why art thou so far from helping me, and from the words of my roaring? O my God, I cry in the daytime but thou hearest not, and in the night season, and am not silent" (KJV). This psalm is a searching description of human depression and despair, of God-forsakenness and terror. Yet it ends on a note of confidence in God's ultimate victory and salvation. Jesus had made the Psalms a central part of his spiritual life, and it makes perfect sense that he should recall this one at the hour of his greatest need. In that final moment the "dark night of the soul" that mystics of all religions have described—the sense that God Himself is absent, uncaring, deaf to one's prayers—came upon him. He felt utterly alone, rejected by both God and humankind. In the dreadful intensity of that despair it seemed his ministry and mission had failed. The Father he had so trusted now appeared a mirage and a delusion. Small wonder Luke omits this cry of dereliction, as it is often called; small wonder John's Gospel, with its majestic view of Jesus—in charge even on the cross—omits it as well.

Yet I have always felt that we are on very holy ground at this point. The episode must be authentic because, again, it is one you would never willingly invent or include unless the truth forced you to do so. The evident embarrassment of Luke and John supports this view. But it is at this time of greatest weakness and stress in Jesus' life that we can most identify with him. If even he, with his deep awareness of the reality and presence of God, could experience this hell and yet be vindicated, there is no human hell of suffering—mental, emotional, physical or spiritual—to which his message and witness are irrelevant. That he honestly and fully knew the kind of prayer that is wrung from the human heart when it is breaking or already lost in its own sense of abandonment says more to our pilgrimage of faith than all the later dogmatic attempts to make him a god. The idea of the Second Person of a Holy Trinity knowing what it is to be God-forsaken has only to be stated to be recognized as absurd.

The full version of what has come to be known as the Lord's Prayer—"Disciples' Prayer" would be more apt, since it was really the prayer Jesus gave his disciples to use—is found only in Matthew. Luke has the prayer, but in a shortened, perhaps more primitive form (compare Matthew 6:9–13 with Luke 11:1–4). In Matthew, Jesus first of all gives a few general rules about prayer. When you pray, don't be like the hypocrites "who live to be seen by others praying in the synagogues and in the public squares"—they will be rewarded appropriately. Instead, go into your closet and, shutting the door, pray to your Father in secret, for He sees what is done there; He Who sees in secret will reward you. Avoid empty, repetitious phrases such as the heathen employ, who think they will be heard better, the more words they use: "Be not like them, for your Father knows your needs before you ask." It should be noted in passing that some commentators (with whom I agree) believe the words about entering your closet refer, in characteristically parabolic style, to that secret place within oneself where one can commune alone with God in silence.

Then Jesus tells his followers to pray like this:

"Our father, you who are in heaven,
May your name be kept holy,
May your kingdom come,
And your will be done on earth as it is in heaven.
Give to us our bread day by day
And forgive us debts as we have forgiven those who have
    wronged us.
Lead us not into the time of testing.
But deliver us from every evil."[2]

This is not the place to elaborate fully on meaning. Here again the point is that Jesus gives no indication whatever that this prayer should be addressed to himself. It is clear from the entire tone and setting that the idea of such a thing would have scandalized him. The prayer implies we too are to have great intimacy with the "Ground of our being"[3] whom we are to address as our Father or Parent. He exists in "heaven"—not some remote, inter-galactic "place" but a spiritual plane or "divine dimension." What we have is a statement of God's transcendence or otherness and, at the same time, of His immanence or nearness to and in human hearts and lives. His

name is to be hallowed or kept holy—duly reverenced in all
we say, think, or do. The prayer that His Kingdom may come
does not contradict other sayings to the effect that God's reign
is already at hand or within our innermost selves. It has yet
to come in all its fullness. Though its signs are everywhere, it
still awaits the hour when all people recognize and acknowledge it for what it is. As long as there is still injustice, war, or
other misery upon the earth, to that extent it has not yet been
fully born or realized. Each of us has his or her part to play.

In the prayer for daily bread is contained, by implication
or extension, a request for all our physical and material needs
to be fulfilled. The emphasis is on needs; there is no encour-
agement to pester God with our wants. The petition for forgiveness of our trespasses or debts is characteristically made
conditional on our readiness to forgive others and their
slights, real or imagined. And here Jesus is touching on a
deep spiritual truth; it is very doubtful whether anyone who
is not prepared to forgive others can really know what it is to
accept forgiveness for himself or herself. The two final
clauses, about temptation and deliverance from evil, should
be understood primarily in the context of Jesus' belief that
the final testing or end-time tribulation was about to begin.
One prays to be spared that time of apocalyptic terror and to
be delivered from every danger. Our modern application of
these words to less spectacular trials is nevertheless entirely
natural and valid.

Luke's chief contribution to understanding prayer in the
life and teachings of Jesus comes in Chapter 11, where he
presents a shorter version of the Lord's Prayer. We are then
told a parable stressing the need for perseverance in praying,
which concludes: "And I say to you, ask and it will be given
unto you, seek and you will find, knock and it will be opened
unto you. For everyone who asks, receives, he who seeks,
finds, and to everyone who knocks it shall be opened" (9ff.).
To this point, he has seemed to be saying that prayer is indeed
an open, blank cheque, even a kind of magic—say the right
words, keep it up long enough, and your reward is automatic.
But what follows makes the meaning clear. Jesus points out
how earthly parents, with all their faults ("being evil") still
know how to give good things to their offspring when they

ask for them: "How much more," he says, "will your heavenly father give the *Holy Spirit* [some early manuscripts say "the Good Spirit"] to those who ask him." The parallel passage in Matthew reads this way: "How much more will your heavenly father give *good gifts* to those who ask." Luke's account reflects his own special interest in God understood as active and present by His breath or spirit (Greek *pneuma*). The Spirit is not some Third Person of a Trinity or some separate entity. It (she, he) is God unseen but dynamically present in the lives of human beings—and particularly in the life of Jesus himself.

Luke is in essence telling us that the supreme prayer, the best thing we can ever request, is for God's Spirit—that is, God Himself—to come and work, dwell, and move within us and all we do. It is a prayer that is never refused, Jesus promises. For me this entire passage is one of the most encouraging and enlightening in the whole Bible. Before the cross and Resurrection, long before the elaborately worked-out theology of the fourth and fifth centuries, and some twenty years before St. Paul's famous letters, Jesus was telling those who would hear that God is more anxious to give of Himself, His Spirit, His indwelling presence and power, than we are to ask for it. That, I believe, is good news.

On Holy Communion

In the middle of the sixteenth century, three of the most brilliant and dedicated bishops in the history of the Anglican Church were burned at the stake in Oxford, England. Bishop Hugh Latimer and Bishop Nicholas Ridley were executed on October 16, 1555, and on March 21 the following year the Archbishop of Canterbury, Thomas Crammer, the chief architect of the Anglican *Book of Common Prayer,* met the same fate. Their "crime" was their steadfast refusal to accept the medieval doctrine of Transubstantiation. This long and ominous-sounding term denotes the dogma that at the precise moment when the priests consecrate the bread and wine at Holy Communion the "whole substance of the bread and wine" is turned or converted into "the whole substance of the Body and Blood of Christ." The "accidents"—the appearances of bread and wine—remain, but the underlying substance is miraculously changed. The communicants thus receive the Real Presence of God in their hands and mouths. The fact that the Sacrament of Communion is meant to be a feast of Christian love apparently had little power to deter the bishops' executioners, nor did the absence of biblical evidence for their case: there is not a single piece of justification for the dogma of Transubstantiation in the New Testament itself. Indeed, the word was never even heard of for the first ten centuries and only makes sense in terms of the philosophy of the pagan Aristotle as reinterpreted by Thomas Aquinas in the thirteenth century.

I have written elsewhere of the scandalous fact that the Lord's Supper—intended to be a means of experiencing unity among Christians—has become the point on which the churches are still most keenly divided.[4] Thus, for example, even though the Roman Catholic and Anglican (Episcopal) theologians on the joint international commission set up originally by Pope Paul VI have reached total agreement on what the Eucharist actually means, members of the two communions are no nearer being able to share at each other's altars than they were centuries ago. The more orthodox a denomination, the more eager it seems to be to forget Christian love and bar outsiders from its purported "fellowship meal." What concerns me here is the massive violence and bloodshed that has taken place over what began as a very simple ceremony of remembrance. It is my conviction that what has happened to and around this rite is a paradigm of what has happened to Christianity as a whole. The distortions of Jesus' original intention and action at his last meal with his disciples become starkly apparent once you strip away all you know about Holy Communion from other sources and examine the original text.

The earliest written account of the supper is found in St. Paul's first letter to the Christians in the port of Corinth; the tradition recorded in Mark obviously goes back to the historical Jesus. But Mark was written down about A.D. 66, while Paul's letter was composed ten or fifteen years earlier. Paul writes: "For I received from the Lord that which I handed on to you, namely that the Lord Jesus, on the night he was betrayed, took bread. And, having given thanks [to God] he broke it and said: 'This is my body broken for you. Do this in remembrance of me.' Similarly, when they had eaten dinner he took the cup, saying: 'This cup is the new covenant in my blood. Do this as often as you drink it in remembrance of me.' For as often as you eat this bread and drink the cup you make known the death of the Lord, until he comes" (I Cor. 11:23–6). It is interesting to note the context in which Paul is writing. He has heard of excesses at the Lord's Supper in Corinth: some people at the service have pushed themselves forward to eat and drink up ahead of their fellow members. The result has been that "one member is left hungry while yet another is drunk. Do you not have your own houses to eat and drink in? Do you despise the assembly of God?" (vv. 20–1). Clearly there is no question of the elaborate ritual the Holy Communion was eventually to become smothered in; Paul is simply warning against such down-to-earth matters as greed and drunken debauchery. There is nothing to suggest that only very special people could officiate at the holy meal, or that God Himself was being consumed.

In Mark's account the time of Jesus' betrayal was the night of the Passover (15 Nisan) when all pious Jews ate the sacrificial lamb and unleavened bread to commemorate the night on which their forefathers escaped from Pharoah's Egypt in the liberation of the Exodus. After the eating of the lamb, the head of the house would take the flat bread, distribute it to all, and say, "This, the bread of affliction which our fathers ate . . ." Then the cup of blessing would be passed around. Anyone today who has been present at a Seder meal knows the context in which Jesus instituted his new "supper." Mark's version differs very little from that of Paul, so we have two independent sources that are mutually corroborative. The fourth Gospel, John's, omits the actual institution of the Supper by Jesus, replacing it with the washing of the disciples' feet. John also differs on the chronology here: he sets Jesus' betrayal on the night before Passover (14 Nisan), at the time the lambs for the celebration were actually being killed.

Jesus himself probably knew no Greek. Since he would have spoken Aramaic, the Semitic-type language of Palestine in his day, we know he must have taken the unleavened bread, held it up before breaking it in pieces for all to share, and said: "This, my body. This cup, my blood." Aramaic would not supply the word "is" in either case. Given that he is patterning his words on the Passover words—"This, the bread of affliction," and so on—we can infer he meant to say only that the bread represented his body and the cup of wine stood for his blood. To the objective reader there is nothing to suggest Jesus meant that either the bread or the wine literally was or contained his actual flesh and blood. He was using the symbolism in the Passover meal to illustrate a new covenant of forgiveness and liberation between God and humanity, to be sealed by the sign of his self-giving sacrifice of love. Still less is there any suggestion here—or elsewhere in the entire New Testament—that he was instituting a literal sacrifice of his body and blood to be offered and reoffered by a special caste of holy men to be known as sacrificing priests. There are no grounds for the crude, not to say cannibalistic, ideas behind the medieval dogma of Transubstantiation. This active, effectual remembrance of his voluntary offering of himself in death is intended to be a bond of unity between all who would follow as his learners or disciples, a pledge of the indissoluble link of forgiveness and love between God and all humanity.

As Jesus himself was later elevated to Godhead and full divinity, and as the perennial attraction of the old religion—the possibility of doing something to get right with God—continued to assert its power, the rite gradually became invested with a sacrificial and supernatural aura obscuring the simple beauty of what Jesus first did. At the center of the forces that eventually built a monument of divisive dogmas and taboos and rituals around the Lord's Supper can be discerned the all-too-human lust for power. To have the power to make God appear on the altar, with ringing of bells and swinging of censers; to have the unique authority to offer up before the heavenly throne the ultimate sacrifice, God Himself as the Second Person of the Holy Trinity; to be able to offer the faithful none other than the living God upon their tongues—there is no headier (or more potentially deadly) role than this. One could kill to keep it undefiled.

And so it was that the whole violence-prone mystique about

the Mass or Eucharist arose. Excommunication—to be cut off from this bloodless sacrifice—became the most terrifying threat of all. The executioner could kill only the mortal body, but the power of excommunication could send a soul to hellfire for eternity. And here lay the power of priests, bishops, and popes. Next to the stranglehold exerted on the faithful by its all-pervasive teachings about sex, there was no stronger lever in exerting the will of the Church over those whom Jesus had come to liberate from the fetters of guilt and man-made religion.

I used to feel very moved when celebrating the Holy Communion. The so-called Real Presence for me was the way in which God came by his Spirit into the hearts and minds and lives of all those who were truly seeking to have him dwell there. The bread and wine were powerful symbols of our deep oneness with each other and with our heavenly Father. The remembrance of Jesus' death became the instrument whereby we all were challenged once again to follow his example of loving and serving others, even to our own cost and possible "crucifixion." In the simple act of eating and drinking together—what could be more ordinary?—we were brought to see the holy in the common everywhere around us. The bread and wine were no empty signs pointing to a spiritual reality; rather, just as the exchange of wedding rings effectively conveys what it symbolizes, so the offering and accepting of bread and wine became a pledge between God and the individual that what he or she was seeking was really being received in the "inner person." I was particularly conscious of the way God accepts us regardless of our past, our "warts," our limitations, as I went down the rows putting the fragments of bread in the communicants' hands. Young hands, old hands, smooth hands, hands gnarled and worn by labor and care—each pair told its own story, and together they silently made the most eloquent prayers I ever heard. Now that I no longer take services as a priest, I cannot say I miss being the one in charge—though many priests tell me this is what they would miss most if they ever left the ordained ministry. But too often the long, wordy ritual masked the reality of Jesus' intentions more than I could bear.

Today I go to Holy Communion less frequently, but—provided I can shut out the inevitable churchy perambulations at the beginning and most of the less relevant prayers—I still find the Sacrament a great source of strength. It confirms the Jungian insight that deep down all humans are connected, one, and then lifts that communal perception to join in still deeper oneness with the source of all our beings, God. Sharing in one loaf and drinking from one cup in Jesus' name still seems to me a central part of what it means to be a Christian. But there is nothing here of priestly power or special preserves for special castes. I see no reason why whenever two or three Christians, or more, come together to worship, they should not choose one of their own number to preside at the sacramental meal. There is nothing in Jesus' teaching to forbid such a celebration, and certainly nothing to prevent the celebrant from being female. In the last analysis, the attempt to keep women out of the priesthood comes down to a fear of losing male privilege and power.[5]

On Non-Violence

Theological romantics are fond of looking back at the Church in the earliest days and attributing idealistic purity of faith and practice to its "undivided" members. The truth is that there never was a time when what is now accepted as orthodoxy was held *semper et ab omnibus ubique*—always, by everyone, in every place. As Professor L. S. Greenslade of Christ Church College, Oxford, has pointed out, "that early unity and catholicity were never absolute, except by definitions which have not stood the test of time; and an uncritical admiration for the early Church is little more justified than a one-sided devotion to the Medieval Age of Faith, or a godly reformed Church."[6]

Just as the views of who Jesus was (and is) in the New Testament itself differ, so too did Christology in the centuries that followed. What is perhaps most disconcerting to the lay person who has uncritically accepted the myth that the early church was an idyllic, problem-free community with a single creed, is the extreme violence that all too often prevailed in the battles over developing doctrines and the struggles for churchly pomp and power. Today we are keenly aware of the

scandal of Protestants warring against Roman Catholics in
Ulster or of Maronite Christians (under the rule of Rome)
battling Muslims for control of Lebanon, but this religio-
political violence has an ancient, shameful ancestry indeed.
Greenslade underlines this point with a description of a horrific episode in Rome, near the end of the fourth century, in
which Christians slaughtered Christians over who should be
pope. When the deacon Ursinus was consecrated instead
of his rival Damasus, the latter "stirred up by bribery all
the carriage-drivers and the ignorant mob, and, armed with
sticks . . . broke into the Julian Basilica and rioted there for
three days, *with much slaughter of the faithful.* A week later, he
took possession of the Lateran Basilica with all the faithless
party, and had himself made bishop." He then made some
further bribes, had Ursinus sent into exile, and "began to use
force upon the laity of Rome who would not join him, beating
them with sticks and attacking them in other ways." When his
opponents rescued seven presbyters and took them to the
basilica, "Damasus and his band of traitors gathered the glad-
iators and grave diggers *and all the clergy,* with axes and swords
and clubs, and besieged the basilica. . . . Some of his servants
began to unroof the church and to kill the . . . people with
the tiles. Then all Damasus' party broke into the basilica,
killed 160 of the people, men and women, and wounded a
very large number, of whom many died."[7]

This account, drawn from contemporary sources, is obviously partisan—as in most history, it depends on who is
telling the story. The unorthodox or "unfaithful" are always
those on the other side. Nevertheless, all sources agree that
this dispute over papal power was conducted with the utmost
cruelty and much loss of life. And it is but one example
among many. In other words, following the marriage between
Church and empire under Constantine, Christian violence
was not confined to attacks on non-believers; it quickly spilled
over into the realm of ecclesiastical politics and theological
disputation. Since these developments occurred at a time
when dogma about the person of Jesus was being hotly de-
bated, they tend to support the thesis that Christianity has
always cared more about affirming an absolute God-Man-
Christ than about trying to hear and do obedience to what he

said or commanded. However academic our approach to the Gospels is, it cannot be denied that in his core teaching Jesus advocated non-violence and practised it himself to the very end. You cannot square the Sermon on the Mount with any theory of war, even a so-called "just war." It is particularly significant in our own time that support for nuclear arms and, in some cases, for a nuclear "first strike" comes from Christians of the fundamentalist right who pride themselves on their "loyalty" to the Word of God and the full deity of Jesus. If you study their literature and listen to their preaching, you will find they say very little about the content of Jesus' teaching in the Gospels at all. They much prefer the Pauline writings, especially Romans 13 with its call for obedience to the state and "the powers that be." They also like the Book of Revelation, but fail to heed the warning of its thirteenth chapter—that the state can very easily become demonic in its abuse of power.

In general, it must be said that Christians of all parties and denominations have failed to come to terms with the full meaning of Jesus' words about non-violence—except, of course, for Quakers, Mennonites, Hutterites and others in the tradition of total pacifism. What is true of non-violence as a whole is even more so when we consider the most original, most revolutionary pronouncement Jesus ever made: "You have heard that it has been said you shall love your neighbor and hate your enemy. But I say to you, love your enemies and pray for those who persecute you that you may be children of your Father in heaven. Because he makes the sun arise on the good and the evil alike and sends his rain upon the just and the unjust. For if you love those who love you, what reward have you? Do not tax collectors do the very same thing? And if you love your brethren only, what credit is that to you? Do not the gentiles do the same? Therefore, be perfect [in love] as your heavenly Father is perfect [love]" (Matt. 5:43–8).

At first sight this seems an impossible ideal, and certainly most preachers down the ages have taken it as such. The only problem is that Jesus was not an idealist: he was a pragmatist, an ethical realist in the extreme. He speaks of morality not as a set of rules laid upon humanity from the skies but as a description of the inner laws of the cosmos. He teaches from the perspective of one who has seen that any ethical principle, particularly the root principle of love, becomes an "I ought" as a result of an "is." This *is* the way the universe works, he says, not, Do this because I say (or some other authority says) you should.

Ironically, it is the contemporary crisis over nuclear weapons and the real threat of a global holocaust—just at a time when God's will for a united human family is also potentially within our grasp—that throws Jesus' words about loving our enemies into a fresh and compelling light. At the moment one thing is certain: if we continue in our present state of spiritually stunted growth, if we contine to play "us and them" in a global confrontation with our "enemies," some kind of catastrophe awaits us and our planet. We need more than anything an intellectual and—above all—a spiritual leap forward if a fiery Armageddon is to be avoided. We need to see that all the traditional thinking about "us" and "our enemies" has been a way for humanity, through its political rulers, to avoid dealing with the real issues thwarting its true development and destiny. As long as there is an enemy, real or imaginary, states can always sidestep dealing with oppression and injustice at home. As long as there are those we hate, we can each project onto the "other" all the conflicts and weaknesses we are unwilling to confront in ourselves or in our society. What quickly becomes apparent, when you ponder the matter, is that those who become obsessed with the enemy, personal or political, are ultimately fated to grow into the likeness of the very thing despised. Jesus was deeply aware that one becomes *like* the object of one's hatred. In a war, however "just" each side believes it to be, it soon becomes impossible to tell which power is the most barbarous. Atrocity soon matches atrocity, and morality itself becomes the most tragic casualty of all. Thus in our bid today to match or surpass the nuclear might of the "tyrannical" Soviets, we create ever more devilish weaponry whose only purpose is to threaten the most absolute and final abrogation of human rights ever conceived by humankind.

Loving your enemies does not mean being stupid, naive, or cowardly. Jesus was none of these. It does mean willing the best for them; it does mean dropping all the hostile stereotypes and seeing them as objects of God's love; it does mean taking the initiative in seeking peace with them. It means, above all else, taking a radically new outlook and approach—abandoning fear. God knows, our age-old way of handling international tensions hasn't worked before, and for it not to work now could bring the end. Jesus' way, on the other hand, has never yet been tried. It's time it was.

JESUS AS PROPHET

How the Disciples Saw Jesus

*A*ND JESUS went out, and his disciples, into the towns of Caesarea Philippi: and by the way he asked his disciples, saying unto them, Whom do men say that I am? And they answered, John the Baptist: but some say, Elias [Elijah]; and others, One of the prophets. And he saith unto them, But whom say ye that I am? And Peter answereth and saith unto him, Thou art the Christ. And he charged them that they should tell no man of him" (Mark 8:27–30, KJV).

In northern Israel at a place called Banias (after the Greek god Pan), one of the three sources of the Jordan River bubbles out of the rock at the foot of Mount Hermon. For Christians this place has pivotal significance because it is traditionally associated with Peter's great statement of his faith that Jesus was the promised Messiah. In the later, fuller account of Matthew, Peter adds to "Thou art the Messiah" the words "the Son of the living God." Matthew also provides the reply that is so crucial to the Roman Catholic view of Peter as head of the early Church and the first pope: "Blessed art thou, Simon Bar-jona: for flesh and blood hath not revealed it unto thee, but my Father which is in heaven. And I say also unto thee, That thou art Peter [the Greek word for a rock] and upon this rock I will build my church; and the gates of hell shall not prevail against it. And I will give unto thee the keys of the kingdom of heaven . . ." (16:13–20, KJV).

Protestant scholars argue that the rock upon which Jesus here says he will build his church is the faith expressed by Peter rather than upon Peter personally, and there are now many Roman Catholics who concede that this is the more likely interpretation.[1] It certainly appears, as Matthew continues, that Peter's position is far from anything envisaged in later teaching about the papacy. In verse 23 Jesus rebukes him harshly: "Get thee behind me, Satan: thou art an offence unto me; for thou savourest not the things that be of God, but those that be of men."

What concerns us here, however, is not to settle ancient quarrels between denominations, but to discover how Jesus' own disciples saw him. They had lived with him intimately for nearly three years (if we accept that as the length of his ministry) and when he asked them how he was perceived, they answered that most people took him for one of the prophets. Even Peter did not view him as God in human form—otherwise he would scarcely have dared to try to talk his Master out of going to Jerusalem to death and resurrection, nor would his later denials of even knowing Jesus make very much sense.

In fact, if you read Mark's whole Gospel carefully you will discover that the disciples were far from recognizing the divinity later attributed to Jesus. The very ones who should have been most able to see through the "disguise" are at times depicted as dull-witted and even downright stupid. They understand little of what is being said, let alone who Jesus is supposed to be. All of the Twelve forsook him at the crucifixion, and at first none of them believed the story of his Resurrection. The original ending of Mark is lost to us, but the oldest manuscripts we have end this way: "And they went out quickly and fled from the sepulchre; for they trembled and were amazed; neither said they any thing to any man; for they were afraid" (16:8, KJV).

Some scholars, indeed, have calculated that Mark deliberately showed the disciples in a rather bad light because he was conscious of a serious problem. If Jesus was the Son of God in the later, more orthodox sense, how was it that his closest associates—the witnesses of his miracles and the confidants of his deepest teachings—never knew who he was until well after the Resurrection? The first three Gospels, especially Mark (1:44, 5:6), frequently show Jesus telling those he has healed of demons not to make his identity known. According to the scholars (mainly German) who propounded this idea of the "Messianic secret," Mark invented the device to explain why Jesus' true identity was concealed from those who heard him preach and saw him heal.

Of course Mark does not consider the other possibility—that the Jesus created by the faith of the early Church was not fully compatible with the actual, historic Jesus. True, the disciples were baffled by his person, his role, and his teaching. But the evidence indicates that they never dreamed of him as God Incarnate because the concept itself had not yet been invented. It would have been as inconceivable to them as to Jesus himself. After all, it was he who said: "Call no man good. There is one good, namely God" (Matt. 19:17).

So we come back to the statement in Mark that Jesus' contemporaries saw him as a prophet. Since, apart from John the Baptist, there had been no recognized prophet in Israel for at least two hundred years—it was a common lament at the time of Jesus that the voice of authentic prophecy had been taken away from God's People—the title of prophet was no small thing. Some, Mark says, even thought of Jesus as The Prophet, the one who was to come as a second Elijah to usher in the Day of the Messiah.

The Two Strands

At this point it is helpful to look briefly at the role of the prophets in the Hebrew religion. They are commonly believed to have been mystical individuals able to foretell the future, but this is a distortion. They were mystical enough, men with a clear vision of the nature and being of God; often, like Amos, they came in from the wilderness with a stern message of impending judgment. Yet as the Greek words (*pro phetes*) behind their name indicate, the prophets' function was not to foretell but to "tell forth" the word God had laid on their minds and hearts. It is true that they often speak of punishments or retributions about to fall on the Jewish nation. But their canvas is painted with very broad strokes. They are men who can "read the signs of the times" and discern in the present the consequences that will almost inevitably follow. I say "almost inevitably" because the whole point of the prophets' utterances was to persuade the people to repent and so avoid the evils otherwise certain to come. They laid no claim to detailed predictions of the future, as some modern psychics do. Instead, they applied to the religious, social, and political situations of their time their reading of God's character and will. Any falling short of this standard, they warned, could only result in disaster. And the various disasters they announced were all implicit in the particular situations then facing the Chosen People of God.

The great thing about the prophets is their insistence that experience and knowledge of God come not from cultic, religious piety—from sacrifices, offerings, and ritual observances administered by priests or other intermediaries—but from a direct encounter with a living reality. Their authority comes not from organized or institutionalized religion but from their own direct sense of calling from God Himself. Amos expresses it thus: "The Lord has spoken [to me]; what can [I] do but prophesy?" (3:8). It was this sense of immediacy and directness in knowing God that brought the prophets into sharp and constant conflict with the other strand in Hebrew religion, the cultus or organized worship that was the preserve of a special caste of people, the priests. In Solomon's time this worship came to its fruition in the Temple. From the very earliest days, however, Judaism had worked out an elaborate system of taboos, rules, and rituals to be observed in the proper worship of the Almighty. The Temple, first Solomon's and later that built by Hezekiah and completed by Herod the Great, became the hub and focus of this impressive cult. God had to be propitiated through due observance of the religious code. The "keys" to this kingdom lay in the hands of the priests, particularly those of the High Priests who entered once a year on Yom Kippur into the Holy of Holies to make sacrifice and atonement for the sins of all. In this way, access to God is not immediate and direct but is mediated to humankind by others set apart and chosen tribally for such a function.

Now, the important thing to remember is that all the major steps forward in the understanding of Who God is and what He is really like, what He desires His people to be and to do, came from the mouths of the prophets. Let us be quite honest. Many of the images of God in the pre-Christian Bible—the Old Testament—are crude, vengeful, and immoral. God is often pictured as an angry, arbitrary, bloodthirsty tribal deity more concerned with his own "honor" and privileges than with human well-being. It is to the prophets (and the Psalmist) that we owe the concept of God as a loving, forgiving, peace-seeking Lord who longs for His "children" to return and find pardon and wholeness (salvation). It is to the prophets that we are indebted for the stirring vision of God's desire for justice and mercy for the oppressed and needy of the earth. It is the former herdsman Amos who cries that God cares nothing for burnt offerings and the "noise of solemn assemblies" while injustice flourishes. He writes as the word of God: "But let judgment run down as the waters, and righteousness [right dealing, fairness] as a mighty stream" (5:24).

Reread Isaiah in a modern version, and you will be struck forcibly by the way he flays his contemporaries for putting on extravagant displays of religiosity while ignoring or cheating the poor. Instead of elaborate rituals, he warns, God wants just relations between all sorts and conditions of people: "Learn to do well; seek justice, relieve the oppressed, give justice to the fatherless, plead for the widow." Significantly, forgiveness is available full and free—without the High Priest: "Though your sins be as scarlet, they shall be white as snow; though they be red like crimson, they shall be as wool" (1:16–20).

Not surprisingly, there is almost always an acute tension in the Bible between the priestly or cultic and the prophetic. The priestly establishment, with its privileges, its prestige, and its enormous power over people's souls, naturally reacts with horror to anyone who comes unbidden, without proper credentials—tribal lineage, training, or official recognition—and dares to speak in the name of God against those who are supposed to be the religious specialists. Their response, not just in biblical times but throughout the ages, has been one of shock, anger, and, eventually, violence. Most of the prophets, as the Epistle to the Hebrews reminds us, died horrible deaths at the hands of the allegedly holy. In like manner Jesus himself was destined to be murdered at the hands of the Romans and at the request of the High Priest. The traditional religious establishment always honors the memory of the prophets in the centuries afterwards, but the prophets themselves are cut down. They threaten too much. If God is to be known in acts of justice and mercy rather than in rituals, if He reveals himself without the intervention of the sacred apparatus and its officials, if He forgives without sacrifices, then the entire hierarchy and its raison d'être are called into question. The whole edifice could come tumbling down.

When we consider the two strands in Hebrew religion (and to some extent the distinction applies in other religions as well) it seems obvious that Jesus was firmly on the prophetic side. Clearly he stressed that religious ceremonies devoid of truth in the inner part—that is, not matched by concrete behavior and way of life—were worse than useless. He does not ignore the Temple or the cultic side, but the thrust of his message is for the reality of an immediate encounter with God and for the deeds that must of necessity always flow from the same. His strongest condemnations, like those of the Old Testament prophets before him, are always directed at the professional holy men. Religious hypocrisy is far worse than the sins of harlots and tax collectors. Those who make a great show of their religiosity and piety go into the Kingdom of Heaven after those they consider sinners.

In his encounters with the Pharisees, the sect that tried so hard to observe every part of the ritual code, Jesus affirms his connection with the prophetic tradition by quoting often from Isaiah. When, for example, the Pharisees criticize him and his disciples for eating without first observing the necessary ritual washings, Jesus replies: "Well hath Esaias [Isaiah] prophesied of you hypocrites, as it is written, This people honoureth me with their lips, but their heart is far from me. Howbeit in vain do they worship me, teaching for doctrines the commandments of men. For laying aside the commandment of God, ye hold the tradition of men, as the washing of pots and cups; and many other such like things ye do. And he said unto them, Full well ye reject the commandment of God that ye may keep your own tradition" (Mark 7:1–9, KJV). Then, in a style characteristic of the Gospels' view of him, and wholly in line with the prophets, he goes radically beyond their external piety to the inner, spiritual core of the matter: "There is nothing from without a man, that entering into him can defile him; but the things which come out of him, those are they that defile him" (v. 15).

Luke takes the theme of Jesus as prophet even further, showing Jesus at the very outset of his ministry speaking in the synagogue at Nazareth. Standing up to read, he chooses a passage from Isaiah: "The Spirit of the Lord is upon me, because he hath anointed me to preach the gospel to the poor; he hath sent me to heal the brokenhearted, to preach deliverance to the captives, and recovering of the sight to the blind, to set at liberty them that are bruised [downtrodden], to preach the acceptable year of the Lord." Sitting down in the traditional role of the rabbi or teacher, he continues: "To-day has this scripture been fulfilled in your ears" (4:17ff., KJV). By putting this episode at the beginning of the public minis-try, Luke gives us his version of Jesus' program of action, his understanding of what it was Jesus came to do. As we will see, the passage is of critical importance for a contemporary understanding of who Jesus is for us. For the moment, though, it is enough to establish the prophetic mode as one in which Jesus felt completely at home.

If any doubt remains, one has only to read what follows in the Lucan account. Hearing his claim to fulfill the role de-scribed by the prophet Isaiah, the hometown congregation is full of wonder and, to some extent, shock. They say to them-selves, "Is this not Joseph's son?" (v. 22). In other words, be-lieving they know his roots, they are amazed both by the gra-ciousness of his speech and by his audacity. Sensing their problem, Jesus says: "Surely you will tell me this proverb—'Physician, heal thyself; do in your own country the things we have heard you have done in Capernaum.' But truly I tell you, no prophet is accepted in his own country" (vv. 23–4). Then, driving the point home, he goes on to remind them of par-allels from the lives of two of the famous prophets of old, Elijah and Elisha.

Even in the fourth Gospel, with its highly developed understanding of the person of Jesus, there are primitive traces of the view of him as a prophet or, indeed, the great eschatological Prophet who would precede the Messiah. In Chapter 3 Nicodemus refers to Jesus as a rabbi and "teacher come from God." After the miracle of the loaves and fish (6:1ff.), the crowd begins to say, "This is of a truth that prophet that should come into the world" (KJV) and verse 16 shows that some wanted to make him king. In the next chap-ter (7:40ff.) this concept is repeated: "Many . . . said, Of a truth, this is the Prophet. Others said, This is the Christ. But some said, Shall Christ come out of Galilee?" Finally, the blind man whom Jesus healed tells the Pharisees: "He is a prophet" (9:17). (In fact, the miracles performed by Jesus are themselves another link with the prophetic tradition—see below, pp. 63–8.)

An End to Religion?

Now, given the abundant evidence that not only his contemporaries but Jesus too thought of himself as a prophet of God—though as we shall see he was also much more—it is interesting to see how Christianity has reversed the situation. The organized religion that professes to follow Jesus has treated him as though he were firmly on the side of the cultic or priestly approach to God, the Living Water. The Church has made itself out to be the supreme dispenser of Grace, or the Presence of God's enabling Spirit. While Jesus' message was one of immediacy, of universal, direct access to his Father, of forgiveness full and free to any who asked, the Church has set itself up as the mediator between God and human beings; instead of immediate access we have a hierarchy of priests, bishops, and archbishops standing between ourselves and God. Naturally the Church proclaims Jesus the supreme mediator—though he never claimed this for himself—but then it makes him so distant a figure that a host of other mediators is required as well: the Virgin Mary, an army of special saints, and, of course, the pope. At the time of the Protestant Reformation, in the sixteenth century, the recovery of the Bible as the final arbiter of faith and morals meant that many of these obstacles were swept away. Yet the renewal was incomplete. The Bible itself was set up as a mediator—along with Christ—between the believer and his or her God. At the same time, proclaiming that forgiveness and salvation come by faith alone (*sola fide*), Protestantism made repentance and faith or conversion a kind of "work" or meritorious action essential for salvation.

The truth of the matter is that Jesus came, in a very radical sense, to abolish religion and all the ritualistic paraphernalia it puts in the way of knowing God. To understand my meaning, think for a moment about the nature and essence of religion itself. *Religio,* the Latin word we translate as "religion," is made up of two elements: *re* (again or afresh) and *ligio* (indicating a tying or binding together, as in "ligament"). What religion is basically about is the attempt by humankind to renew its bond with God. Essentially the term describes our efforts, through rites, creeds, pomp and ceremony, to heal the sense of brokenness or alienation we feel at the very source of our being. There is an almost universal awareness that in some way we are removed from our true spiritual home; in theological terms, we have all sinned and come short of the glory of God. The problem with religion is that it actually worsens the situation it was meant to correct.

Before showing how this comes about, it is worth noting again that in ancient Rome the name for the high priest was *Pontifex Maximus. Pontifex* means bridge-maker; thus the high priest was the chief bridgebuilder between man and God, carrying out the main work of *religio* by offering sacrifices to reunite God and man through the propitiation of God's wrath. In the same way the pope as Supreme *Pontiff* allegedly holds the keys that determine who is to find reconciliation with God and who is not.

The problem with religion is that in its all too human efforts to make peace with God it cleaves human reality right down the middle. It tears apart more than it heals. Above all, it divides life into the sacred and non-sacred: these things, actions, vestments, places, words, times, and people are sacred or holy; the rest are secular or profane. Thus we have the disastrous body-soul dichotomy in religious history, a dichotomy that even today shows its results in the negative ecclesiastical understanding of sex and the body. The obsession of the Church, especially the Roman Catholic Church, with sexuality; the rules about celibacy, divorce, birth control; even the issue of women's ordination—all these are results of the split. The reason the Church of the Middle Ages and later was able to do such cruel things to people in the name of Jesus lay in the belief that the body itself was either evil or worthless. The Inquisition's torturers considered the pain they inflicted to be of little account compared to the glory of saving an eternal soul.

Moreover, as Dietrich Bonhoeffer often pointed out, religion also seeks special privileges for itself—wealth, power, prestige. From one very important point of view, the whole of organized religion is a not-too-subtle form of power-seeking and control. One reason sex has always been so crucial to ecclesiastical dogma is that it is the intimate point at which human beings are most susceptible to controls imposed from outside. Our capacity for imposed guilt leaves us very vulnerable to manipulation by others.

Reflecting on Jesus' life and teaching, I can't help but conclude that most of the apparatus of institutionalized religion is a contradiction of his central mission. He came talking not about religion but about life, not dividing up reality but affirming its essential unity, calling us not to power and prestige but to lowly servanthood. Jesus was not laying down rules or setting up castes of holy mediators so that we might find God. He came affirming that forgiveness is full and free now to any who will turn to receive it. As in the parable of the prodigal son, the Heavenly Father is not to be bought over by rituals but is already waiting for our return long before we even realize we have been "lost." Religion always wants to stress what we must *do* to gain wholeness or salvation. Jesus' message is, Relax, trust—the Kingdom of God is at hand, even within you; you have only to be conscious of this to enter fully in.

It is profoundly interesting that while parts of the New Testament speak of Jesus as a priest or high priest—there is no mention at all of a special caste of Christians who are ever to be called priests—he never speaks of himself in those terms. He sees himself as shepherd, rabbi or teacher, prophet, and master, but never in the role of one who stands pleading between us and God. Nor does he anywhere in the first three Gospels say that one must wait until some distant date—say, after his crucifixion and Resurrection—either to be forgiven or to receive God's presence, the Spirit, within. Forgiveness is present now as a datum of the universe created by his Father. God gives the Holy Spirit to anyone who asks, more readily than any father would give bread to his hungry child.

THE FOURTH GOSPEL

T HE VAST differences between the Gospel According to St. John and the first three, or Synoptic, Gospels have been commented upon by Christian scholars all the way back to the Church Fathers of the second century. Clement called it "the spiritual Gospel," and Eusebius the historian said it was written to supplement the first three with additional material on the early part of Jesus' ministry. But the disparity is actually much greater than that—with John we are in an almost completely different world. And the differences are not simply a matter of additional or "spiritual" content.

There are, for example, clear differences of chronology. In the first three Gospels, the cleansing of the Temple comes at the very end of Jesus' ministry and actually precipitates the crisis leading to his "trial" and murder. In John this same event is placed firmly at the beginning of the public ministry and is clearly meant by the author(s?) to symbolize the truth that Jesus' mission is to purify and cleanse the faith of Israel. Ultra-conservatives who insist on literal interpretation claim that there must therefore have been two cleansings of the Temple, but this is ducking the problem, not solving it. There are other time differences too, including the dating of the Lord's Supper or Eucharist, and even the length of Jesus' ministry itself.

While Mark has no birth narrative at all, beginning his account with the ministry of John the Baptist, Matthew and Luke each have a "Christmas story" as well as a genealogy. By contrast, John says nothing of Wise Men or Bethlehem but instead starts with a remarkable Prologue that sets Jesus' coming on a cosmic plane. The Word made flesh (John 1:14) is the same Word that was in the beginning with God. In fact, this Word is God. He is the agent of creation. There is no mention here (or anywhere in this Gospel) of a Virgin Birth; this coming is of an eternal being who becomes human although he is really the "only begotten of the Father"—the unique Son of God (though verse 12 clearly states that Jesus' followers are also given the "power to become the sons of God").

The Johannine Prologue, then, warns us from the outset that this Gospel will be radically different in tone from the others. Instead of introducing Jesus as a hidden Messiah, or one reluctant to reveal his true identity—as in the first three—John presents him *immediately* as Son of God and King of Israel. Thus unlike the Synoptics, which require us to wait until Peter's confession of faith in Jesus as Messiah at Caesarea Philippi, John has a rather obscure convert, Nathaniel, blurt out a much stronger statement of orthodoxy right in the first chapter (1:49). Jesus strides across the stage as a majestic figure confident from the start that he is the Son of God. Talking to the Samaritan woman at the well, Jesus has no hesitation in telling her he is the Christ: "The woman said to him, I know that the Messiah is coming, which is called Christ; when he is come, he will tell us all things. Jesus said to her, I that speak to you am he" (4:25–6).

The significance of these disparities cannot be stressed too strongly. While there are some obviously primitive historical elements in this Gospel (which show that parts of the tradition it is based on go back, if not to the disciples themselves, at least to a source close to them), nevertheless its understanding and portrayal of the person of Jesus in no way synchronizes with that of the Synoptic Gospels. Scholars, who have written whole libraries on this problem, recognize a number of stages in the molding of this Gospel. It was probably completed in its present form between A.D. 90 and 100. Its Christology is not that of the earliest disciples during Jesus' earthly ministry but rather that of the post-Resurrection Church. In other words, it is a reading back into the life of Jesus of beliefs formed after the first Easter. Some experts believe that much of the actual discourse material—the long passages where Jesus is made to sound more like a Greek philosopher than a Jew in Palestine (see, for example, Chapters 15 and 16)—had their origin in prophecies or ecstatic utterances by charismatic leaders in the early Church. Thus the open claims to unique Sonship are to be seen not as utterances of the historical Jesus, but as statements of later dogma placed on his lips. This would explain why, for instance, the absolutist claim (which has led to Christianity's "theology of hostility")—"I am the way, the truth, and life. Nobody comes to the father but by me" (14:6)—is not recorded by Matthew, Mark, or Luke. It is something the historical Jesus never uttered.

If you read the parables in the first three Gospels and then compare this apparently characteristic teaching technique with the way John has Jesus speak, you once again recognize that we are dealing with two quite different accounts of what happened. We cannot have it both ways. Jesus either spoke the way Mark reports it (4:34), in pithy aphorisms, parables, and other stories, or he taught in the lengthy, spiralling—even convoluted—major discourses recorded in John. The styles are mutually incompatible.

The treatment of Jesus' miracles is also vastly different in the two camps. John tells us that the miracles are "signs"—in other words, their function is to throw light on who he is and what he has come to do. Thus John places the seven (the number itself symbolized perfection) signs of his Gospel at strategic points.

For example, the miracle of changing the water into wine at the wedding in Cana (2:1ff.) does not appear to be based strictly on historical fact. It is recorded only in the fourth Gospel—since Peter and the others were there, it is odd that Mark should be silent about such an event—and seems to play a quite deliberate part in the evangelist's plan to set forth Jesus and his teaching as superior to the old order of Judaism: to compare the two is like comparing wine with water; Jesus, like Dionysus in Greek mythology, gives to life new color, warmth, and joy. Indeed, John quite pointedly says the six huge stone pots that were filled with water at Jesus' command and that when poured out provided wine that was much better than what was already being served—"You have kept the best wine until the last!" exclaims the surprised ruler of the feast—were pots used for ritual cleansings "after the manner of the purifying of the Jews" (2:6). It is this Jewish ritual that Jesus, in John's view, eclipses and transforms. He goes on to say this was the first miracle or sign that Jesus performed, because he wants to set the whole of the ministry in this context. The story in this same Gospel of the raising of Lazarus from the dead is another example, notorious for the difficulties it presents. This seventh and last of the Johannine "signs" that Jesus is said to have "shown forth" is not in Mark, Matthew, or Luke. Again we have the problem of why this is so, since such a miracle, if it really happened, would have become very widely known. It is difficult to believe that the resurrection of so close a friend of Jesus would have not featured largely in, say, the preaching of Peter, and so have found its way into Mark's Gospel. Added to this problem is the fact that the risen Lazarus neither says nor does anything worthy of record. Finally, whereas the first three Gospels present Jesus' cleansing of the Temple as the final provocation for the authorities, John plainly says it was the raising of Lazarus, with the conversions that resulted from it, that precipitated the crucifixion: "Then from that day forth they took counsel together for to put him to death" (11:53, KJV). One can only conclude that John's chief purpose in placing and telling the story is theological. It is a sign of Jesus' own Resurrection and provides the opportunity for the saying: "I am the resurrection and the life. He that believeth in me, though he were dead, yet shall he live" (11:25, KJV).

These examples should be sufficient to show why the fourth Gospel cannot be taken literally when it has Jesus making extraordinary claims for himself. We are dealing here not with history but with theologizing by those who have come to faith in the Risen Christ. And this is of key importance when we consider that John's Gospel was to become the main source of dogma about the person of Jesus in subsequent centuries. Beginning with what was already the product of a sophisticated theology, the Church Fathers took the process at work in it through to its final dogmatic conclusion.

THE ACTS OF THE APOSTLES

MODERN SCHOLARS generally date the Acts of the Apostles, the fifth book of the New Testament, at somewhere between A.D. 80 and 90. The work itself claims Luke, the traveling companion of St. Paul, as its author, and there seems little reason to doubt this. Our particular concern, however, is with the Christology that Acts sets forth. Acts is of great significance for this enquiry into who Jesus was because it contains undisputed evidence of the content of the early preaching of the Apostles themselves. I find no reference here to a Divinity, pre-existent with and part of God from the beginning, who comes down to visit earth for thirty-three years (or whatever figure you set for Jesus' life), is put to death, rises again of his own power, and returns to his original place as Second Person of the Holy Trinity.

In Acts Jesus is always subordinated to "God"; he is raised from the dead not by his own innate power as God, but because "him hath God raised up"; and he is generally spoken of in a manner much more supportive of the Arian position (i.e., Jesus seen not as the eternal Son but as created by God to be His agent in creation, etc.) than of anything resembling traditional orthodoxy.[1] Certainly he is proclaimed as Lord (*kurios*), the Messiah or Christ, and the Son of God, but none of these titles means that Jesus equals or is God. Listen to the Apostle St. Peter right after the first Pentecost: "Ye men of Israel, hear these words; Jesus of Nazareth, a man approved of God among you by miracles and wonders and signs which God did by him in the midst of you, as ye yourselves also know . . ." (2:22, KJV). Notice that Jesus is spoken of *as a man approved by God;* the signs or miracles were performed *by God* using Jesus as His agent or emissary. Verse 24 makes it plain that it was God who raised Jesus from the dead: "Whom God hath raised up . . ." This fact is stated twice in verse 24—and reiterated throughout the bulk of the New Testament. Another key assertion is added in verse 36, when Peter says, "Let all the house of Israel know that *God hath made that same Jesus,* whom ye have crucified, *both Lord and Christ.*" The emphasis must be placed on the words "God hath made" Jesus both Lord and Christ: if he was made to be Lord or Master and also Messiah, to place him on the same rank of divinity as the living God is near blasphemy.

This is not an isolated passage in Acts. The very next incident is the healing of a lame man by Peter and John at the gate of the Temple. (In passing, it is worth noting that the two had gone to the Temple to pray: they had as yet no sense of being part of a new religion called Christianity, and saw Jesus as the fulfillment of their Jewish faith.) A crowd gathers after the healing and Peter preaches another sermon (3:1ff.) in which he calls Jesus by a series of titles: the "Holy One" (v. 14), "the Prince of Life" (v. 15) and "Christ." Right in the middle, however, he says this: "For Moses truly said unto the fathers, A prophet shall the Lord your God raise up unto you of your brethren, like unto me; him shall ye hear in all things whatsoever he shall say unto you. And it shall come to pass, that every soul, which will not hear the prophet, shall be destroyed from among the people . . . Unto you first, God, having raised up his Son Jesus, sent him to bless you . . ." (vv. 22ff., KJV).

Jesus is clearly portrayed here as a prophet raised up by God, "like unto me"—that is, like Moses. He is the "prophet" who must be listened to and obeyed. There is an enormous difference between this view and the one that categorically proclaims Jesus is God or vice versa. Thus when the faithful gather together after the healing miracle provokes a run-in with the powerful Sadducees (who were annoyed because the Apostles were preaching life after death—a doctrine they loudly denied) they join in praise to God, the Creator (4:24ff.). There is no thought of praying to Jesus—he is spoken of as "thy holy child," "whom thou has anointed" (4:27). The Greek word for "child" is *pais,* which can also mean "servant." The word for "anointed" is *echrisas,* the root of the title "Christ"—literally, "the anointed one." In other words, what Peter is saying is "your holy servant Jesus, whom you made Christ." This concept of Jesus' complete subordination to God, Who has anointed him or declared him to be Christ, ties in with what Luke tells us in his Gospel was Jesus' own view of his calling: in the first sermon he gives, in Nazareth, Jesus reads from the prophecy of Isaiah about the Servant of God who would come and who would be anointed by His Spirit to proclaim the good news of the Kingdom to the poor and oppressed (Luke 3:17ff.).

In Chapter 5 of Acts the Apostles are brought before the Sanhedrin, the supreme council, to defend their incessant street preaching in the face of orders to desist. Here they say: "The God of our fathers raised up Jesus, whom ye slew and hanged on a tree. Him hath God exalted with his right hand to be a prince and a Saviour. . . ." (vv. 30–1, KJV). Notice again the insistence that God is in control, that He is behind the whole of Jesus' Resurrection and exaltation; Jesus is a human being chosen and exalted by the power of the living God. Later the martyr Stephen, in his speech before his death (Acts 7:1ff.), makes the chief point that the history of the Jews is one of killing the prophets. The slaying of Jesus, the Just One, is the climax of this rebellion against the messengers of God.

In Acts 9:20 we are informed that, soon after his conversion, St. Paul preached in various synagogues saying that Christ was the Son of God. If accurate, this is the first instance of any Apostle's using this formula in a sermon. Most scholars think it may be a reading back into the story of what Paul's views later came to be; this seems all the more likely when we learn, two verses later, that the burden of his early preaching was "proving that this [Jesus] is very Christ." Demonstrating from the Old Testament that Jesus was really the fulfiller of Messianic promises—despite the scandal of having been hanged on a cross in apparent defeat—was the central thrust of all the early preaching to Jewish audiences. The message about his being Son of God did not come until later, when the Apostles extended their mission to include Gentiles. The idea of an anointed Messiah made no sense whatever to non-Jews; the concept of a Son of God, on the other hand, was something they knew very well. For further proof that Paul concentrated at first on showing that Jesus was truly the promised Messiah, one has only to read the account of his sermon in the Jewish synagogue at Thessalonica: "Paul, as his custom was, went in unto them, and for three Sabbath days reasoned with them out of the scriptures, telling them that Christ had to suffer and be raised from the dead, and that this Jesus whom I preach unto you is Christ" (Acts 17:1–3, KJV). The Jews' early rejection of this message was based not on the alleged divinity of Jesus, but on the unacceptable idea that the Messiah had been murdered by the Romans and God's People.

Before leaving Acts, I would like to look briefly at the famous passage where St. Paul, in Athens, stands on Mars' Hill and preaches, using as his text the inscription on the alter there "To The Unknown God". Paul, who could adapt his message to any audience, quotes the Greeks' own poets to remind them that they also are the offspring or children of God. He tells the people it is time to repent of their idolatries and warns that God has a Day of Judgment coming when everyone will be judged "by that man whom he has ordained; whereof he has given assurance in that he has raised him from the dead" (17:31). Notice that he calls Jesus "that man whom [God] has ordained." The Greek word that the King James Version translates as "ordained" is *horizo,* meaning set apart, appointed, or separated from others for a special task or status. In other words, Paul says that God designated Jesus for his special mission and future. Of course, in his letters to the various churches, Paul shows scant interest in Jesus of Nazareth, the historical Jesus; he is much more concerned with his own theology and with the Christ of faith.[2] Nevertheless, it is significant that the Book of Acts ends with the following description of his ministry: "And Paul lived in his own hired house [in Rome] for two whole years and welcomed all who came to see him, *preaching the Kingdom of God,* and teaching those things which concern the Lord Jesus Christ, with all confidence, nobody forbidding him" (28:30–1).

THE MIRACLES OF JESUS

Miracles in the Old Testament

THE WORD "miracle" is derived from the Latin *miraculum*—an event that causes wonderment because of its unexpected, unusual character. The *Concise Oxford Dictionary* defines a miracle as "a marvellous event due to some supernatural agency, a remarkable occurrence." That Jesus performed miracles is attested to by all four Gospels (indeed, most of Mark is an account of the exorcisms of demons, the healings, and the nature miracles of Jesus). Those who insist on taking everything in the Bible literally—though even they do so in a very spotty way—maintain the miracles are proof positive that Jesus was God Incarnate. Leaving aside for a moment the question of their historicity, however, we must challenge that contention on a number of grounds.

In the first place, there are miracles of every kind in the Old Testament ascribed to Moses and a number of the prophets. We have healings at a distance, nature miracles in which the forces of nature are apparently changed or controlled by the man of God, and even the raising of the dead. In truth, almost every miracle attributed to Jesus in the Gospels has its counterpart in the Hebrew Bible, yet nobody has made divine claims for any of these miracle workers. A prophet was supposed to be able to command signs and wonders as evidence of his heavenly calling. Thus Moses was able to confound the sorcerers of Egypt with his wonder-working powers; he struck the rock and the waters flowed out when the people were dying of thirst; at his word the sea parted so that the Children of Israel could pass over on dry land, and as they watched, the sea flowed back to engulf Pharaoh's army.

Jesus healed lepers, but so did Elisha the prophet, as we read in II Kings 5:1–14. Naaman, captain of the Syrian forces, was a leper and, on the advice of a young Israelite girl who had been captured and was serving as a maid to his wife, he sought out Elisha. The prophet did not come out to see him but sent a messenger telling him to go and bathe in the

Jordan River seven times. Naaman at first was angry and refused to do Elisha's bidding: "Are not Abana and Pharpar, the rivers of Damascus, better than all the waters of Israel?" In the end, though, he went to the Jordan as he had been told and "his flesh came again like unto the flesh of a little child." A few versus later (6:1–7), we have the story of how Elisha retrieved an axe head that had fallen in the water: he cut down a stick from a tree and cast it into the water above where the axe head sank—and "the iron did swim." But neither of these miracles ranks with the prophet's feat concerning the Shunammite woman's young son—a passage in many ways reminiscent of the story of Jesus' raising of Jairus' daughter. Here it is in the King James Version: "And when Elisha was come into the house, behold the child was dead and laid upon his bed. He went in, therefore, and shut the door upon them twain, and prayed unto the Lord. And he went up, and lay upon the child, and put his mouth upon his mouth and his eyes upon his eyes, and his hands upon his hands: and he stretched himself upon him: and the child sneezed seven times, and the child opened his eyes." The woman was then called in and Elisha said to her, "Take up thy son" (II Kings 4:32–7).

This miracle is an almost exact replica of the one attributed to Elisha's predecessor Elijah, the prophet who had already worked a miracle for the widow with only enough oil and meal left to last one day. Asking her to share these with him, he promised her the supplies would not be consumed until the terrible drought had ended: "And the barrel of meal wasted not, neither did the cruse of oil fail, according to the word of the Lord which he spake by Elijah" (I Kings 17:17ff., KJV). Shortly afterwards, however, the widow's son fell ill, "and there was no breath left in him." Elijah took the boy up to a loft in the little house where he himself lived and laid him on his own bed. Then, after prayer, he stretched himself upon the child three times. "And the Lord heard the voice of Elijah; and the soul of the child came into him again, and he revived." The woman, like many in the Gospels, responded: "Now by this I know that thou art a man of God, and that the word of the Lord in thy mouth is truth."

Miracles of supernatural interference with the laws of nature—comparable to Jesus' command of wind and waves, or his reported ability to walk on water—are also featured prominently. The most familiar example is in the account of the conquest of the promised land, Canaan, by Joshua and the Children of Israel. Joshua commanded the sun and moon to "stand still" so that he could have light whereby to see and kill the Amorites: "Sun, stand thou still upon Gibeon; and thou, moon, in the Valley of Ajalon. And the sun stood still, and the moon stayed until the people had avenged themselves upon their enemies." The period is cited as twenty-four hours: "So the sun stood still in the midst of heaven, and hasted not to go down about a whole day" (Josh. 10:12–13, KJV).

A similar, though less well-known, interference with the spinning of our planet around the sun (the Israelites, of course, thought of the sun as moving about the earth) is recorded in II Kings. Hezekiah, the king, asks the prophet Isaiah for a sign that God is going to heal him as promised. Isaiah gives him a choice; he will command the shadow on the sun dial either to move ahead ten degrees or to go back ten degrees, whichever the king prefers: "And Hezekiah answered, It is a light thing for the shadow to go down ten degrees: nay, but let the shadow return backward ten degrees. And Isaiah, the prophet, cried unto the Lord: and he brought the shadow ten degrees backward, by which it had gone down in the dial of Ahaz" (20:8–11, KJV).

Miracles in the Time of Jesus

But it is not just in the Hebrew Bible that miracles, signs, and wonders abound. The Gospels bear ample testimony that Jesus' contemporaries expected anyone claiming to be a prophet or to have some unique mission from God to work healings and other portents. "What sign dost thou work?" is the challenge of the religious leaders when they ask Jesus' justification for cleansing the Temple (John 2:18, KJV).[1] It takes some effort to appreciate how different the presuppositions of the ancient Near East were from those of modern rationalists: the people who watched the historical Jesus saw his actions against a background of belief in actual demons and divine intervention in human affairs.

Jesus' own attitude to his healings and other wonders is also revealing. It is apparent he saw them as evidence that the Kingdom of God was at work in his ministry (Mark 3:22ff.), but at the same time he downplayed them—"Go and tell no man . . ."—because he did not want to be thought of simply as some kind of wandering magician. As Humphrey Carpenter points out, other Jewish figures in Jesus' time did have that kind of reputation: "Honi the Circle-Drawer was said to have brought rain to end a drought, and Hanina ben Dosa supposedly worked miraculous cures, some of them, like the cures of Jesus, being performed at a distance from the sufferer. This indicates that Jesus' reputation as a miracleworker, healer and exorcist was by no means unique. . . . It was part of the vocabulary of the time for expressing how remarkable someone was."[2]

Beare notes that there are "remarkably few references to the miracles of Jesus in the New Testament apart from the Gospels."[3] In other words, the writers knew that in themselves the miracles proved very little. They struck people with amazement and drew large crowds, but they clearly did not result in faith that he was a divinity on earth. They were not even entirely convincing as proof that he was a prophet. Some, indeed, attributed Jesus' powers to Satan rather than to God: "And the scribes which came down from Jerusalem said, He hath Beelzebub, and by the prince of the devils casteth he out devils" (Mark 3:22, KJV). Furthermore, Jesus himself promised his disciples on more than one occasion that they would also perform healings and other signs of the Kingdom, and the evidence of the Acts of Apostles is that they indeed did so (both Peter and Paul are said to have raised the dead and several other cures are reported involving people who were lame, bitten by deadly serpents, and so on).

In fact, all ancient literatures contain stories of wondrous healings and other feats by outstanding personalities. Nor is this simply a relic from more primitive times. Throughout history there have been shamans, medicine men, yogis, and healers of various kinds who have undoubtedly been able to effect astonishing cures. Having covered the phenomenon of faith-healing as a journalist, I am quite persuaded that such "miracles" do occur (sometimes in spite of the character of the healer concerned).

Jesus' miracles, then, are in themselves no demonstration that he was God Incarnate. Before leaving them, however, I would like to comment briefly on the question of their historicity. It is evident from the Gospels that the miracles are included partly because they were so large a part of the earliest oral tradition about Jesus as it was handed down, and partly because they were important theologically: they are signs that the Kingdom really is at hand and at work. This, again, is most explicit in John, where the author weaves the development of the story around the seven "signs."

Keeping this theological use of miracles in view for a moment, then, we can say with certainty that the stories of healings, exorcisms, miraculous feedings, and other marvels passed through many stages of development before reaching their final shape in the hands of the Gospel writers. That many of them were changed, exaggerated—even in some cases invented—is now accepted by the majority of New Testament scholars. Nevertheless, despite all the fine research that has been done in this area (especially by the Form Critics), it is very difficult to say where the truth left off and invention began.

I cannot accept the strictly rationalist view that the miracles are sheer invention and that their inclusion in the Gospels is due to an inability or unwillingness to discern a difference between legend and historical fact. I reject the position that they are to be understood wholly in a spiritual fashion—as if they were allegories dressed up as real events—although there is no doubt that in the preaching of the early Church it was their spiritual or theological importance that meant most. For example, Jesus' calming of the storm and calling the disciples to renewed trust in God was obviously a relevant message for Christian communities facing "storms" of controversy or opposition. The feeding of the multitudes was undoubtedly read or recounted as an illustration not just of God's care for his children, but more specifically of the way He feeds His Church through the Eucharist or Holy Communion. The "opening" of people's eyes or ears or the "unloosing" of the tongues of the dumb in the miracle stories clearly had deep significance in missionary situations where the converts "saw" and "heard" for the first time the good news of the Kingdom and felt empowered to go out themselves to witness to it.

But the tradition that Jesus did heal the sick and drive out the "demonic" forces believed to oppress those afflicted with mental and emotional illnesses is too primitive and too pervasive in the Marcan account not to have its roots in actuality. I have no doubt that in the charismatic, powerful presence of Jesus people were dramatically healed. We can use all kinds of modern terms to try to explain this phenomenon, but most of them explain very little—we speak of the power of suggestion, of psychosomatic healing, or of the placebo effect as if these themselves were fully understood. The truth is there is a mystery at work in all non-medical healing, which neither doctors nor scientists have as yet been able to rationalize away. Carpenter rightly warns against the attempt to delete entirely the miraculous element in Jesus' ministry: "If we label the miraculous element as fiction and discuss Jesus purely in terms of his teachings we may be satisfying the demands of modern minds which do not accept the supernatural, but we are doing violence to the historical record. We are also leaving ourselves with a 'non-miraculous' Jesus whose extraordinary impact on his contemporaries becomes inexplicable. His teachings on their own are not enough to explain the impression he caused. A more honest historian will say that undoubtedly the miracle stories in their present form include a large measure of elaboration and invention; but he will also say that something happened which gave rise to those stories."[4]

The matter of which stories or parts of stories constitute the "elaboration" may be pursued in numerous specialized studies. What I would like to point out here is how easily we may recognize some of the forces at work in the mythologizing of Jesus' mighty acts. We have already seen how powerfully the Old Testament shaped the interpretation of who Jesus was and is. Prophecies were re-read and given new content as the disciples eagerly strove to prove how he fulfilled them all. Thus if it was expected that the Messiah would open the eyes of the blind or free those made captive by the powers of evil, Jesus must be shown to have done so. If Moses fed the Israelites with "bread from heaven"—the manna—in the wilderness, then Jesus too must feed the crowds miraculously. It is no accident that Jesus performs this feat in a desert or wilderness setting: it echoes the Moses narrative. In the same way Matthew has Jesus give the Sermon on the Mount—the new law or Torah—on a mountain top. As a Second Moses he recapitulates the first giving of the law on Mount Sinai, simultaneously fulfilling and surpassing it.

THE TITLES OF JESUS

The Messiah and the Son of God

EVEN A cursory reading of the New Testament reveals a bewildering variety of names and titles for Jesus. Clearly Jesus and the belief in his Resurrection made such a profound impact on the Apostles and the first recipients of their preaching that they had to call on the highest categories in their tradition to express its meaning. In this, of course, they were also influenced by the need to communicate their good news in terms the people to be evangelized could understand. To Jewish audiences, therefore, they spoke of Jesus as a prophet and the promised Messiah, while to Greek and Roman audiences, who knew and cared nothing about Jewish Messianic concepts, they presented Jesus as "Son of God" and *Kurios*, or Lord. (In fact, the very earliest Christian creed consisted of the words *Kurios Christos,* Christ is Lord).

Historically, the fact that Jesus is given such names in the Gospel and other New Testament traditions has been taken by the Orthodox as bedrock evidence, even "proof," that he was indeed God Incarnate and believed himself so to be from the outset of his ministry. Unfortunately for this hypothesis, except in John's Gospel Jesus seems very reluctant—and in some cases refuses—to claim these titles for himself. He did not go around calling himself the Messiah, though I believe it is evident enough that he thought of himself as fulfilling a Messianic role, one totally different from that popularly conceived of by his contemporaries. Nor did he call himself the Son of God. Luke's account of the irregular trial of Jesus before the Sanhedrin is illuminating. His accusers asked him: "Are you the Christ? Tell us. He replied, If I were to tell you that, you would not believe it . . . Hereafter the Son of Man shall sit on the right hand of the power of God. Then they all said, Are you then the Son of God? He said to them, You are the ones saying that I am" (22::67–70). In Mark's account Jesus responds to most of the accusations at the trial with total silence. However, when he is asked by the high priest if he is the Messiah, "the Son of the Blessed," he replies: "I am; and you shall see the Son of Man seated at the right hand of the power and coming with the clouds of heaven" (14:62).

The point to notice here is that when Jesus is finally forced, as it were, to say whether or not he is the Messiah, he openly admits it but at once speaks of himself as the "Son of Man." This odd term, as we shall see in a moment, is throughout the first three Gospels Jesus' preferred way of referring to himself—not as Messiah, king, savior, Lord, but as *a* or *the* Son of Man.

But aside from the evidence that Jeus did not go about making extravagant claims for himself, there is a much more important issue to consider here. In applying to him terms such as these, were the Gospel writers stating outright that Jesus was God? The answer assuredly is in the negative. To claim to be, or to be called by others, "Messiah" is by no means the same thing as claiming to be or being thought of as God-in-the-flesh, on a par in every way with the Deity. We know this to be the case from our knowledge of Jewish teaching about the Messiah at the time: it was not technically blasphemy to make a false claim to this title. The Messiah as the ideal king or the direct agent of God's ultimate will—to vindicate His people, the Jews, and set up a kingdom on earth where all injustices would be done away with and peace would reign forever—is at times pictured as a superhuman figure, but never as God's equal, never as essentially God Himself. The scrolls from the Essene community near the Dead Sea speak of two messiahs, one priestly and the other a king. Neither was seen or spoken of as God.

We have already seen that at Caesarea Philippi, Peter made his confession of faith that Jesus was the Messiah or Christ; yet almost immediately afterwards he began telling Jesus how to run his ministry. None of the Gospel material following his confession makes any sense at all if you accept the position that to have faith in Jesus as Messiah means believing he is God Himself: in particular, it would not make sense for Peter to deny his Master three times, or for the disciples to forsake him and flee at the crucifixion.

The same is true of the title "Son of God." In the Old Testament the phrase is applied to Israel as a nation committed to doing God's will. For example, Hosea 11:1 reads: "When Israel was a child, then I loved him and called my son out of Egypt" (KJV). An earthly king set apart to do God's bidding could also be called God's son. Thus the prophet Nathan is told by God that King Solomon is to be known as the son of God: "He shall build a house for my name [the Temple] and I will establish the throne of his kingdom forever. I will be his father, and he shall be my son" (II Sam. 7:13–14). In Psalms 2 the conquering king who will be God's Messiah is specifically called by this name: "I will declare the decree: the Lord hath said unto me, Thou art my Son; this day have I begotten thee." The angels too are referred to as sons of God in Genesis, when "the sons of God came in unto the daughters of men" (6:2–4) and in the strange passage that sets the stage for the trials of Job: "Now there was a day when the sons of God came to present themselves before the Lord, and Satan came also among them" (Job 1:6). (Satan, whose name means "the Adversary," comes as one of the angels of God whose office it is to oppose men in their pretensions to a right standing before God.)[1]

But the conclusive evidence that to be called God's son does not mean one is God comes from the mouth of Jesus himself. In Chapter 10 of John's Gospel he tells his religious critics that the Hebrew Bible itself names "gods" and "sons of God" all those whom God has called to serve him and to whom He has revealed Himself. Thus it is only appropriate that he whom God has set apart and sent as His agent should also call himself the Son of God (vv. 33–6); the text he cites comes from Psalms 82:6: "I have said, Ye are gods; and all of you are children of the most High." The fact that this passage appears in the Fourth Gospel—with its emphasis on the doctrine of the Incarnation—makes it all the more important. Indeed, this Gospel makes it clear that the whole purpose of Jesus' ministry was that we might all become fully the sons (and daughters) of God ourselves (1:12).

We have already had cause to look at John's Gospel and to note that it is entirely different in "feel" from the earlier three.[2] John's Jesus seems to be human—for example, he suffers thirst at the well in Samaria—but this aspect is overshadowed by his personal sense of majesty and control in every situation. In fact he strides the earth, boldly proclaiming himself Son of God, the only way to the Father, from the opening page. That this portrait represents a later mythologizing of the primitive accounts is evident to all but the most determined of fundamentalists. The author has taken the title Son of God far beyond anything intended by the term in the Old Testament and closer to the contemporary Hellenistic view of gods who make their appearance in the guise of humans. Yet I must emphasize again that the author is always at pains to portray Jesus as completely subordinate to the Father. Verses such as "He that hath seen me hath seen the Father" and "I and my Father are one" are often cited to prove Christ's divinity, but even here Jesus is not claiming to be metaphysically of the same essence or person as God. In the first, he simply states that in him we can see a vision of God; that he reveals what God is truly like—as far as humans can grasp it. In the second he states powerfully his own conviction that he is united in mind and spirit with the purpose and will of the Father; this passage comes immediately before the verse quoted above, in which he says that all who are called to God's work can be called "gods" or "sons of God."

In John 14:12, after once again declaring that he is "in the Father," Jesus makes a startling assertion: "Truly, truly I say unto you, he that belives on me, the works [miracles] I do he shall do also; and greater works even than these he shall do" (KJV). This is scarcely the message of one convinced his calling as God's Son is so unique as to make him utterly "other" than his disciples. The difference he conveys is one of degree rather than of kind. Those who follow him, he admits, may well perform even greater miracles or signs than he has.[3]

Finally, I want to call to your attention one more passage that raises sharp difficulties for those who insist that the Jesus of John's Gospel is unmistakably portrayed as God Incarnate. It is the theological exchange (4:7–26) between Jesus and the Samaritan woman, at the end of which he acknowledges himself to be the Messiah. The woman brings up the quarrel between Jews and Samaritans over the site where true worship is to be offered to the Lord (the Samaritans contended for Mount Gerizzim, while the Jews, naturally, argued for Mount Zion in Jerusalem), and Jesus tells her a time is coming when it will be at neither spot: "You worship you know not what: we know what we worship; for salvation is of the Jews. But the hour is coming, indeed is already here, when the true worshippers shall worship the Father in spirit and in truth: for the Father seeks such to worship him. God is Spirit: and they that worship him must worship him in spirit and in truth." By including himself in the "we" who worship God and clearly stating that God is Spirit, Jesus refutes all those who would later assume that he claimed to be that divine Spirit himself.

The Son of Man

Significantly, while Jesus never called himself God, and was extremely reticent even on the matter of his Messiahship, he did repeatedly use one enigmatic phrase: "the Son of Man." Even in the crucial passage in Mark when he asks his disciples "who say ye that I am?" and Peter makes his confession of faith—"Thou art the Christ"—Jesus urges silence about that name and goes on immediately to refer to himself not as the Christ but as the Son of Man: "And he began to teach them that the Son of man must suffer many things. . . ." (8:29–31, KJV).

Although scholars have wrestled with this term, found in the Gospels only on the lips of Jesus himself, for well over a century, it has been a particular focus of debate and controversy in the last few decades.[4] The most recent—and most sensible—book on the subject is *Jesus Son of Man* by the great scholar Barnabas Lindars. He concludes that the words "Son of Man," which in the Aramaic spoken by Jesus would have been rendered *bar enasha* and in classical Hebrew *ben adam*, did not amount to a Messianic title in Jesus' own day. Meaning simply "a man," a human being, it was a roundabout, somewhat idiosyncratic way of referring to oneself without saying "I." Since it appears in some of the oldest sayings attributed to Jesus in the Gospel tradition, there can be little doubt it is authentic. And its riddle-like "feel" fits well with his overall style of speech—parables, paradoxes, and ironic one-liners. Take, for example, his saying in Matthew 8:20 (Luke 9:58): "Foxes have holes, and birds of the air have nests, but *bar enasha,* The Son of Man, has nowhere to lay his head." Lindars rightly says that the phrase here means "a man such as I," one called to be God's agent in proclaiming the good news of the Kingdom with its attendant demand for a renewal of personal, social, and religious life. He comments that "the generic bar enasha is a device whereby Jesus can refer ironically to his position as one called by God without making exaggerated claims about himself."[5] He also suggests that the term may have been a means of avoiding the misunderstandings bound to surround Jesus' use of any popular Messianic titles, all of which carried the wrong kind of expectations—the immediate overthrow of the Romans by a politically triumphant warrior-king, for example.

Jesus eludes every attempt to define him in preconceived religious concepts. After his death and Resurrection, a wholly new understanding of Messiahship became inevitable—a Messiah who announces God's Kingdom as already here and yet still to come in power, who appears to fail when he is cruelly done to death, but who is vindicated and raised to be "the leader of those who are ready for God at his coming."[6] It was the earliest Christians, trying to come to grips with this story, who began to weave around Jesus every exalted Messianic concept available, until soon even the authentic expression "Son of Man" came to be loaded with overtones it never had in Jesus' own usage. Like "Son of God" it was stretched to denote a supernatural, heavenly being whose humanity was more seeming than real.[7]

THE DEATH OF JESUS

MOST PEOPLE, churchgoers or not, are familiar with the old hymn "There is a Green Hill Far Away" by Cecil Alexander (1818–95). The last stanza runs

There was no other good enough to pay the price of sin;
He only could unlock the gate of heav'n and let us in.

Chorus

O dearly, dearly, has he loved! And we must love him too,
And trust in his redeeming love, And try his works to do.

This is a popular but nonetheless classic statement of the traditional orthodox view of Jesus' suffering and death. The cross is seen as part of God's plan, from the foundation of the world, for taking away the world's sins and opening the way to eternal life here and in the age to come. Jesus, regarded as God's literal son, morally perfect in every way, is considered the only sacrifice "good enough" to atone for or "pay the price of" sin. He becomes the fulfillment of all other sacrificial victims. His "blood" cleanses the believer from the every stain. As the third verse states, "He died that we might be forgiv'n, He died to make us good,/That we might go at last to heav'n, Saved by his precious blood."

In the eighteenth century, William Cowper (1731–1800) wrote the famous evangelical hymn "There is a Fountain filled with blood, drawn from Emmanuel's veins/And sinners plunged beneath that flood lose all their guilty stains." Set to a vigorous and well-loved American melody of unknown origin, the hymn haunts my earliest memories of going to church, and the mere sound of it still makes me want to be part of a vast congregation of people singing their hearts out. It reminds me of Elisha Hoffman's similarly rousing "Are You Washed in the Blood of the Lamb?"—if you have ever heard a Salvation Army band raising the rafters with the chorus to that one, you know what I mean. In fact, it is unfortunate but true that some of the very best hymns—for singing—in Christian worship belong to this genre. Take "The Old Rugged Cross," or "There is Power in the Blood" by Lewis Jones (1865–1936):

Would you be free from the burden of sin?
There's power in the blood, power in the blood.
Would you o'er evil a victory win?
There's wonderful power in the blood.

Chorus

There is pow'r, pow'r, wonder-working pow'r in the blood of
  the lamb;
There is pow'r, pow'r, wonder-working pow'r in the
  precious blood of the lamb.

The rank crudity of the blood references is off-putting to most middle-of-the-road and liberal Christians, and so you won't find many of these extremely evangelical favorites in their hymnaries. But the concepts behind such songs of praise permeate the whole of orthodox liturgy and theology. Sin, with which the entire human race is infected—even a newborn baby, so the thinking goes—has incurred the wrath of a God so righteous He cannot look at it. Nothing can stay this anger except a spotless being who can serve as the perfect sacrifice or atonement inadequately prefigured in the animal sacrifices of the Temple in Jerusalem. God therefore sends His only Son—part of His very Being—to take upon his own head all the sins that ever have been or ever will be committed. Jesus alone is "good enough to pay the price of sin." He stands in the prisoner's box condemned in your place and mine and dies as a substitute for us.

Theologians down the ages have done their best to make sense of this idea with various theories of the Atonement.[1] I am familiar with most of them and have yet to come across one that ends up with a view of God in any way resembling the Father proclaimed by Jesus himself. At its core, the whole blood-sacrifice myth comes directly from some of the most primitive religious thinking known to the ancient world.[2] It is loaded with anthropomorphisms—notably, the "wrath" or "anger" of a God prepared to see His son murdered to assuage His own passion for righteousness—and suspiciously well-suited to a priestly hierarchy dedicated to perpetuating its own power as the sole agency capable of repeating this sacrifice on behalf of mankind.

Perhaps I am lacking in piety or some basic instinct, but I know I am not alone in finding the idea of Jesus' death as atonement for the sins of all humanity on one level bewildering and on the other morally repugnant. Jesus never to my knowledge said anything to indicate that forgiveness from God could only be granted *after* or *because of* the cross.[3] When the tax-collector Zaccheus announced he was going to give half his goods to the poor and restore any ill-gotten gains fourfold to his victims, Jesus declared, "This day salvation comes to this house" (Luke 19:9). He was constantly assuring his hearers that God forgives all who truly call upon Him in repentance and faith. And in teaching his disciples to pray, he expressly told them to ask for their heavenly Father's forgiveness. This message is the whole point of the three great parables of the Kingdom in Luke 15, particularly that of the prodigal son who returns to find his forgiving father already waiting on the road. The traditional doctrine portrays God as some kind of irascible totalitarian potentate with a vast ledger in which He marks down every conceivable human fall from grace; only the death of His dearest and best can satisfy His fury that we have exercised the freedom He gave us to make mistakes.

This theory is not only crude but immoral.[4] As Jesus taught, this is a moral universe. When we break moral laws we pay for it ourselves, as surely as anyone does who defies the law of gravity by trying to fly off a cliff. Alcoholics or criminals who bring havoc on themselves may well have religious experiences, encounter God, and know forgiveness of all the harm they have done; however, the consequences of their mistakes cannot be undone. The persons they hurt, the damage they do to their own or other people's bodies and lives cannot simply be cancelled out. The burden of guilt can receive healing from God, but He leaves us to work out the rest for ourselves. I find it immoral to suggest that one's "sins" are the responsibility of anyone but oneself. The sins of the Nazis in killing six million Jews can conceivably be forgiven by God. But that does nothing to ease the unimaginable anguish, horror, and grief perpetrated on both the victims and the survivors. I fail to see—even taking the traditional view of Jesus as God Incarnate—how his death could do anything to erase that heinous blot on human history. It seems morally outrageous to suggest that his death on the cross by itself obliterates the "sin" of the Holocaust or any other act of genocide or mass torture—let alone the "sin of the world." In fact, the doctrine of universal forgiveness of sins through the death of Jesus on the cross has very often led professed Christians into a kind of antinomianism, or trivialization of moral error. Since it's all been forgiven anyway, let's sin heartily in order that, to quote St. Paul, "grace may abound" (Rom. 6:1). (Of course, Paul only sets out this perverted notion to rebut it.) This view is a world apart from the experience of those who in the presence of Jesus and his teaching have felt their consciences stabbed and have sought the Lord of Hosts and His forgiveness as they begin their lives again.

Christian traditionalists too easily assume that people of other faiths—for example, Judaism—do not know the experience, the joy of forgiveness from God, or the "Ground of all being." But this is demonstrably false. Jesus himself, whose only Bible was what Christians call the Old Testament, was steeped in the spirituality of the Psalms. These are filled with references to seeking and finding divine forgiveness. One of my favorites, Psalm 103, begins: "Bless the Lord, O my soul: and all that is within me, bless his holy name. Bless the Lord, O my soul, and forget not all his benefits: *Who forgiveth all thine iniquities* [sins]; who healeth all thy diseases" (KJV, my italics).

Having said all this, we must ask afresh what the death of Jesus, the Christ or anointed Agent of God, means for us today. Realizing that there have been many in the course of history who have laid down their lives on behalf of others, and that the Romans crucified thousands of Jews during their occupation of the ancient Middle East, what is it about this specific death on a cross that sets it at the heart of any faith that would be Christian? Why, in the words of "There is a Green Hill Far Away," are we able to say, "We only know it was for us he hung and suffered there"?

The answer lies in our understanding of Jesus' mission as

a whole. Whatever doubts or confusions we may have about this or that verse of the New Testament, there can be no question about its overall testimony to the belief that Jesus, the Messiah or Anointed One, came to make known the inner secret of the cosmos: that there is a Creator God whose essence is forgiving, all-embracing love. His purpose was to communicate this truth in what he said and by what he did—supremely by what he did, because the non-verbal communication of acts or deeds is, ultimately, always the more convincing medium. He taught verbally by means of parables; but his life was in and of itself an acted parable. The word is validated by a life lived. It is sealed by the way he met and triumphed over death.

The hardest thing in life for any of us is to go on trusting that God is love in the face of suffering, especially innocent suffering. There can be no easy remedy. But Jesus is the supreme example of innocent suffering. His witness to us is that even there, even at the point of agony of mind and spirit in which one feels God-forsaken, God's love is never absent. It is the one reality that abides when all seems bleak and dark, and in the end it wins through and over death itself. In the Resurrection, God vindicates Jesus' unconditional commitment to trust in his "Heavenly Father" in the face of the most unjust, God-denying fate any of us could imagine.

What the cross says to us is that there is no experience of life, whether of mental and emotional anguish or of physical pain, where God's redemptive spirit is not also at work. At the same time, it speaks powerfully about the nature of that divine forgiveness. As Jesus hung and suffered there, as he prayed to his Father to "forgive them, for they know not what they do," he revealed that there are no limits to God's willingness to forgive and pardon. Even if in our anger and rebellion there are times when we would like to curse and hit back at God for some real or imagined tragedy in our lives, the cross clarions out that this too can be accepted and forgiven. In a real sense, we can even stand there with those who nailed Jesus to the cross and, in our rage or despair, join in hammering in the spikes. God still forgives. His love is such that there is nothing we can ever do to put ourselves beyond its healing reach.

By willingly accepting the lot of a condemned prisoner, of

a tortured man, and of one disgraced by the ultimate shame, for a Jew, of crucifixion, Jesus identified in death as he had in life with the outcast and rejected in all of human history. Born homeless, for a time a refugee in Egypt, and then, for his brief ministry, a wandering, homeless rabbi who consorted with "publicans and sinners," Jesus forever stands as a champion and servant of the poor, the derelict, the downtrodden, and the marginalized. In being despised and rejected himself, he has affirmed the value as persons of the despised and rejected of this or any age. For individual people and for churches alike, to neglect one's responsibility to these, "the least of my brethren," is to neglect one's Master too. As the great parable in Matthew 25 reveals, to feed the hungry, clothe the naked, and visit the captive is to minister to Jesus himself. So closely did he see himself identifying with the needy that he could say doing a kindness to any of them was to do it to him. Significantly, this parable, which is a word picture of the last judgment, makes acceptance by God dependent not on right doctrine or correct ritual observance, but on having done the will of the Father regarding the poor: "Then shall the righteous answer him saying: When saw we thee a stranger, and took thee in? or naked, and clothed thee? or when saw we thee sick or in prison and came unto thee? And the King shall answer and say unto them, Verily I say unto you, Inasmuch as ye have done it unto one of the least of these my brethren, ye have done it unto me" (Matt. 25:37–40, KJV).

With its vertical thrust towards heaven and its arms thrust out horizontally to encompass the earth, the cross is a powerful symbol or efficacious sign (the true meaning of a sacrament) of on the one hand the deep and abiding unity between God and His creation, and on the other the unity under or in God of all humanity. In this sense, the cross or the death of Christ stands for the Atonement (literally the At-one-ment) of all of us with the Ground of all being. It stands as a pledge of God's unlimited and unconditional mercy and pardon. It "takes away the sin of the world" not because it satisfies some sadistic sense of divine justice, but because it ratifies and sets a seal on the eternal nature of God's forgiveness. We can kneel at the foot of the cross and find, with Pilgrim in Bunyan's great classic, that any burden of guilt we carry has been cleansed or "rolled away." At first thought, the idea that God would, as it were, stand back and allow His anointed servant or "Son" to suffer ignominy and enter into such an experience of weakness and helplessness appears offensive and incomprehensible—as St. Paul wrote, it seemed "scandalous to the Jews and foolishness to the Greeks" (I Cor. 1:23). But to those who see with the eyes of faith it becomes a sign of the power and wisdom of God. His strength is always made perfect through weakness. In our own lives the "Calvary" of suffering or defeat, when seen as an opportunity for God to act redemptively, very often becomes the place of renewal or "resurrection."[5]

While some scholars dispute the Gospel passages that suggest Jesus knew in advance how and when he would die (Mark 8:31, Matt. 16:21–8, Luke 9:22–7), arguing that they are after-the-fact readings back into the text, I believe these are in the main authentic. One could not have the spiritual vision and insight of Jesus and not be aware that the opposition of both the secular powers (the Romans) and the religious authorities (the Sadducees and Pharisees—a strange coalition!) would inevitably lead to confrontation and martyrdom. Jesus' radical call to "seek first the Kingdom of God" was a threat to all those with vested interests in controlling others and preserving the status quo. It is natural that those today who seek to do God's will and establish His Kingdom find themselves similarly at odds with "the powers that be." This kind of situation is most obvious in such places as Central America, South Africa, and the Soviet Union. But it can happen anywhere that Christ's call is truly heard and followed.

Summing up, then, the death of Jesus on the cross is not a matter of an angry deity requiring a perfect offering or sacrifice, a case of one of the "Persons" of God dying to appease the other; nor does it represent some kind of transaction between God and Satan. The cross is at the center of Christian faith now and unto eternity because it is a window into the heart of reality. It reveals the height, depth, and breadth of never-ending divine love and pardon. With its now empty arms, it trumpets forth the victory of the Resurrection in which we all one day shall share. And that is why we can boldly join with St. Paul in saying we are persuaded "that neither death nor life, nor angels, nor principalities, nor present or future circumstances, nor powers—neither height nor depth nor any other thing in all creation—will ever be able to separate us from the love of God which has been shown to us in Jesus Christ our Lord" (Rom. 8:37).

THE RESURRECTION OF JESUS

This Jesus God Has Raised Up . . .

THE FAITH that Jesus, who was crucified, who died and was buried, was later seen alive by the Apostles and large groups of the disciples is the foundation of Christian life and belief. Nobody with the slightest knowledge of the New Testament documents can fail to see this faith as the very heartbeat of the earliest Church, and so it has continued down the ages. As St. Paul says, if Christ was not raised from the dead, we are the most miserable of all people (I Cor. 15:13–19).

I feel wholly at one with that tradition. In studying the New Testament and the history of the early Church, I have examined this Easter faith from every possible angle.[1] That Jesus was given victory over death, that his steadfast trust in his "Father" in heaven was vindicated, that love was proven stronger than the bonds of mortality, that here we receive a foretaste of a glory prepared for each and every one of us— all this I believe with all my heart and mind. Nothing but the experience of witnessing this post-death reality can account for the amazing turnabout that took place in the lives of his followers. At the crucifixion all—except for a few women— forsook him, fled, and hid behind locked doors for fear they would be next on the list for execution. They were defeated and in deep despair. All their hopes had been smashed, their dreams turned into ashes.

Yet in a few days we find the same people preaching in the streets, saying that they had seen and talked with their Master. The authorities threatened them, put them in prison, and eventually put some to death; the first martyr was Stephen. But nothing could stop them. They were seized with an unquenchable sense of joy, of purpose, and of inner power. The Spirit they had seen at work in his life and ministry was now at work in their own lives. They were able to face "the lion's gory mane" in the Roman arenas undaunted, many going to death with psalms of praise on their lips. Against all the odds,

in a few short years they succeeded in turning the world up-
side down, until Rome itself lay vanquished.

These were no victims of mass hallucination, no perpetra-
tors of some preposterous pious fraud. Sane, ordinary people
do not give up everything they own and repeatedly risk their
lives for something they know to be false. I have read scores
of articles and books claiming everything from a plot by Jesus
himself to deceive the authorities to the view of one Muslim
sect that he revived in the cool of the tomb and then fled
eastwards as far as India. (You can still see an ancient tomb
near Amritsar where he allegedly died and was buried at a
very old age). None of these arguments comes anywhere close
to convincing me. I am much more compelled by the earliest
testimony of all, that of St. Paul writing in his first letter to
the Christians at Corinth (about A.D. 53, some ten years before Mark's Gospel was written): "I have handed on the tradition to you at the beginning which I myself received: that
Christ died for our sins, according to the scriptures; that he
was buried, and that he was raised up again on the third day,
according to the scriptures; and that he was seen by Cephas
[Peter] then by the Twelve. Then he was seen by upwards of
five hundred of the brethren at once—of whom the majority
are still alive, although some have fallen asleep [died]. Then
he was seen by James, and then by all the Apostles. Last of
all, as to one born out of due season, he was seen by me" (I
Cor. 15:3–8). It is crucial to note that Paul cites living witnesses—"the majority of whom are still alive"—as proof of
what he is saying. In other words, this tradition is based on
eye-witness testimony that was still available at the time of
writing. He is saying that those who do not believe him can
go and find out for themselves.

But the question we must examine is whether the Resurrection proves that Jesus was God. Does it show that he simply
broke the bonds of death and burst forth from the tomb
triumphant by virtue of his inner "Godhead" or divinity? Traditional Christianity would reply with a resounding "yes."
Hymns, prayers, popular piety—as well as some of the greatest choral music ever composed—picture Jesus as rising from
the tomb and conquering the ancient enemy, death, all by

himself. As even the Apostles' Creed puts it, "The third day he rose again from the dead. . . ."

I believe this is a complete distortion of what the only written evidence we have plainly says. It is the mythology that so quickly surrounded this pivotal event that has warped our vision and made us see something that, on closer examination, simply isn't there. If you listen to the earliest preachers in the Book of Acts or to the authors of the various letters in the New Testament, they are at great pains to proclaim the Resurrection not as an act of Jesus, but as the act of the living God he served. They never say "He rose from the dead"; they say that God raised him up, or more simply, that he was raised up.

In the passage just cited from Paul's witness to the Resurrection, for example, he says that Jesus was "raised up again"; the Greek verb is clearly passive. Or consider the very first sermon in Acts of the Apostles, preached by Peter on the day of Pentecost: "This Jesus God has raised up, a fact to which we all are witnesses" (2:32). In Chapter 4, the account of Peter and John before the Sanhedrin, Peter again says, "Let it be known to you and to all the House of Israel that in the name of Jesus of Nazareth whom you crucified and *whom God raised from the dead,* in this name has this man been set before you whole" (v. 10). This is the very same message—"God having raised him from the dead"—later preached by Paul on Mars' Hill in Athens and wherever the early gospel was made known.

What is being described throughout this early testimony is an event in which God is completely sovereign, completely in control. As the supreme actor in the drama, it is He who vindicates Jesus' trust and commitment unto death. It is He who raises His prophet, agent, servant, and Messiah or Christ from the grave. In every aspect Jesus remains subordinate to His will. This perspective is the very opposite of the Jesuolatry that has so often been part of traditional Christianity and is so prevalent today. Paradoxically, those who most loudly proclaim their devotion to an infallible Bible are the most prone to be unscriptural at this point. They preach a deity who masqueraded as a man and only pretended to die, who had the power of divinity and all creation on his side and loosed the bonds of death himself. In the words of Paul, this is not the gospel, but "another gospel" altogether (Gal. 1:6).

The unequivocal teaching of the New Testament is that Jesus was very much a normal human being. He truly feared death on the cross. He really did die and was buried in the utter helplessness of all humanity. He was raised back to a new dimension and plane of being in the same way all of us will one day be resurrected to eternal life—by a miracle of God's mercy and renewing power. In this sense, he was the pioneer of our future, what Paul calls the "first fruits of them that sleep" (I Cor. 15:20). Let anyone who doubts that what I am describing is primitive Christianity read the description of Resurrection faith in the same chapter. Paul makes it abundantly clear that he believes our own resurrection or entry into the new and higher life after death will be patterned exactly on Jesus' Resurrection. We will be raised not by some innate immortality of the soul, but by an act of God.

This passage is also of key importance for understanding the nature of Jesus' Resurrection. Fundamentalists of all denominations become deeply distressed when one speaks of the Resurrection as "spiritual" rather than physical. For them, a physical resurrection is so basic that to deny it is to put oneself wholly outside the camp of faith. But as Paul himself says while stressing the exact similarity of our resurrection with that of Jesus: "Flesh and blood cannot inherit immortality. This corruptible body must put on an incorruptible body" (I Cor. 15:53)—one fitted for life where there are "many mansions" or, better, many dimensions. It is evident from the four Gospels that Jesus' Resurrection "body" in some ways resembled his historical body; but in many crucial ways it did not at all. Whatever his coming to life again meant, it did not mean the resuscitation of a corpse; he was no longer "flesh and blood," made of human clay. This was an entirely new mode of existence, a new creation destined for another plane of being. You could see him and not recognize him—as Mary Magdalene did, who mistook him for the gardener, or the two disciples on the road to Emmaus, who walked and talked with him without a glimmer of recognition until the breaking of the bread. This new "body" that could pass through closed doors and be in various places at a thought was, if you like, a kind of "soul traveler." It was certainly not the body that had lain in the tomb.[2]

Mythological Elements in the Resurrection Story

I have already stated my conviction that the Resurrection of Jesus is the best-attested fact in the New Testament record. It is at the core of any attempt to penetrate the mystery of his person and his meaning for our time. Yet this truth must not blind us to the reality of another fact—that the Resurrection event, from almost the very beginning, not only shaped the perception of all that was remembered of Jesus' historical existence, but was itself quickly surrounded by mythological overlays and interpretations. The most important of these was the almost immediate assumption that he rose from the dead of his own volition and innate power as God, part of a Triune Deity. But let us turn briefly to some of the other embellishments.

Matthew's Gospel follows the Passion and Resurrection sections of Mark very closely in the main outlines but adds a number of new elements—what Beare calls "legendary embroidery."[3] These are the death of Judas by hanging (27:3–8); the dream of Pilate's wife (27:19); Pilate's washing of his hands and the acceptance of guilt for the blood of Jesus by "the whole people" (27:24ff.) (what terrible persecution and hatred the Jewish people have suffered at so-called Christian hands because of this addition to the tale!); certain sayings of Jesus (26:26–9); and the story of the guard at the tomb (27:62–6). In the latter, for example, Matthew informs us that the Pharisees and chief priests came to Pilate asking for a guard to be set on the tomb "lest his disciples come by night and steal him away, and say unto the people, He is risen from the dead" (KJV). They give as their reason the memory they have of Jesus' saying, "After three days I will rise again." As Beare notes, this is preposterous: none of the Gospels suggests he ever made such a prediction *in public*, and since the disciples themselves seemed to have forgotten he ever said it to them, it is most unlikely that these "outsiders" would know of it at all. The reason for adding the episode, he says, was to counter then-current Jewish allegations that the disciples had stolen the body, and that Jesus was not raised from the dead.[4]

A more obvious example of the mythologizing process is Matthew's account of what happened at the moment of Jesus' death: "And, behold, the veil of the temple was rent in twain from the top to the bottom; and the earth did quake, and the rocks rent; and the graves were opened; and many bodies of the saints which slept arose, and came out of the graves after his resurrection, and went into the holy city [Jerusalem], and appeared unto many" (27:50–3). These elements—the quake and the resurrection of pious Jews—are found only in Matthew. The veil, which closed off the holy of holies from the rest of the Temple, could not be seen by anyone who was not actually inside. Its tearing is not a matter of history but of symbolism: it represents in mythical form the argument presented elsewhere in the New Testament—see Hebrews 10:19—that by his death Jesus opened to all the place where God was thought to dwell. (Only the high priest was permitted to enter the holy of holies, and at that only once a year, on the Day of Atonement; it was so sacred a place that even today very pious Jews refuse to walk anywhere on the Temple Mount for fear of accidently treading where the holy of holies once stood.)

The story of the saints' being resurrected from the tombs to the east of the city, just below the Mount of Olives, and going into Jerusalem is also the result of an attempt to give mythical form to the belief that Jesus was the "first fruits of them that slept." Surely an event of such stupendous dimensions, had it actually occurred, would have not only found its way into other Gospels and letters in the New Testament, but would also have been recorded in some other Jewish or Roman historical source. Yet the record is silent.

Finally, it is worth commenting on the last two verses of Matthew (28:19–20). Here alone in the Gospels do we find any reference to the Trinitarian formula. Jesus tells the disciples, "Go ye therefore, and teach all nations, baptizing them in the name of the Father, and of the Son, and of the Holy Ghost" (KJV). All but the most conservative of scholars agree that at least the latter part of this command was inserted later. The formula occurs nowhere else in the New Testament, and we know from the only evidence available (the rest of the New Testament) that the earliest Church did *not* baptize people using these words—baptism was "into" or "in" the name of Jesus alone. Thus it is argued that this verse originally read "baptizing them in my name" and then was expanded to work in the dogma. In fact, this view first put forward by German critical scholars as well as by the Unitarians in the nineteenth century, was stated as the accepted position of mainline scholarship as long ago as 1919, when Peake's commentary was first published: "The church of the first days did not observe this world-wide commandment, even if they knew it. The command to baptize into the threefold name is a late doctrinal expansion."[5]

GREEK AND JEWISH ROOTS OF THE ORTHODOX VIEW

AS EARLY as the eighth century, the theologian St. John of Damascus frankly admitted what every modern critical scholar of the New Testament now realizes: that neither the doctrine of the Trinity nor that of the two natures of Jesus Christ is explicitly set out in scripture.[1] In fact, if you take the record as it is and avoid reading back into it the dogmatic definitions of a later age, you cannot find what is traditionally regarded as orthodox Christianity in the Bible at all. The view of Jesus as at the same time fully man and fully God was unknown to Jesus himself, and came into being as a result of political forces, time-conditioned philosophies, cultural assumptions, and clashes between specific personalities. Nevertheless, it is true to say that already within the pages of the New Testament we can see at least two strands of reflection on the life, death, and Resurrection of Jesus that made the evolution of the full-blown orthodoxy of the fourth and fifth centuries possible. Before moving on to consider more completely the meaning and relevance of Jesus and his teaching for us today, we must look briefly at these elements and their roots in the philosophy and mythology current in his own time.

The Divine Logos

By the beginning of the Christian era, the best minds in both Judaism and Greek philosophy had long been concerned with the theological problem of how a God who was totally "other," wholly transcendent, could at the same time be involved with or immanent in His creation, and thus present to human beings in an intimate, personal way. At the time of Jesus these debates were still going on, with heavy borrowings on either side. And central to all of them was the concept of the Logos—a Greek term that can mean simply a word or an utterance, but can also mean reason, rational principle, or design.

For the pre-Socratic philosopher Heraclitus (*ca.* 500 B.C.) the Logos was the universal mind or reason pervading and governing the world. Later, the Stoic philosophers adopted the concept and taught that all human beings contain a "seed" of this Logos (*spermatikos logos*), which is the reasoning, vivifying "soul" or "spirit" of each person; since we all share in this common source of light and life, we are all members of each other in one cosmopolitan world. The term was then taken over by the Jewish and Greek intellectuals of Alexandria—the university city where much of the later thinking about Jesus as God-Man developed—and the Logos came to be seen as a kind of intermediary agent between God and His world. Of that group of thinkers, the most relevant for us is the Jewish philosopher Philo, a contempoary of St. Paul who was heavily influenced by Greco-Roman thought, especially neo-Platonism and Stoicism. Philo taught that God's Logos— His reason or Word—was His mediator in creation and in all His relations with the world. This Logos was not only "God" but also "Man," and men, he said, aspire to be children of "God's Man, who being the Word of the Eternal must himself be imperishable." Philo also called the Logos God's "firstborn," the "eldest" of the angels. As the heavenly Man or Ideal Human, the Word was the express image of God who acts as His viceroy, imparting revelation: "God the Shepherd leads his flock in accordance with right and law but setting over it his true Word and *first-born son.*"[2]

The parallels between this kind of language and the opening verses of the fourth Gospel are striking: "In the beginning was the Word, and the Word was with God, and the Word was God. The same was in the begining with God. All things were made by him; and without him was not anything made that was made. In him was life, and the life was the light of men. . . ." (KJV). Consider also the opening verses of the letter to the Hebrews: "God, who at sundry times and in divers manners spake in time past to the prophets, hath in these last days spoken unto us by his Son, whom he hath appointed heir of all things, by whom he made the worlds; who being the brightness of his glory and the express image of his person. . . ." We cannot prove direct borrowing, but it is obvious that the authors of these New Testament passages shared with

Philo a common thought-world of Hellenized (Greek-influenced) Judaism.

But the Greek Logos concept was not the only influence on Jewish thinking about the relation of God to His world. Philo and others connected the Logos to developments within the Jewish tradition itself regarding God's Word as His agent in creation—as in Genesis 1:3: "And God *said*, Let there be light, and there was light"—and particularly to ideas then emerging about the Wisdom of God as a personified divine mediator. In the Book of Proverbs we find Wisdom personified (the theological term is "hypostatized") and are told how she was possessed by God in the beginning, was brought forth before creation, and then acted as His helpmate in laying out the foundations of the earth (see, for example 2:6 and 3:19). Frances Young shows how in the later, non-canonical books of Ecclesiasticus and the Wisdom of Solomon this concept is developed further.[3] Wisdom becomes the first-born of all creation, and "a kind of Stoic Logos, the immanent spirit of God, 'pervading and penetrating all things.'" She is described as "a clear effulgence of everlasting light, an unspotted mirror of the working of God and an image of his goodness." In other words, what began as an attribute of God—His wisdom—has become semi-independent, "acting as God's agent." Other writers conceived of the Torah as being the same as God's Wisdom; the two coalesce in the projection of a pre-existent divine figure. There is an almost exact parallel to this Logos-Wisdom thinking in the Epistle to the Colossians, another major source of the later God Incarnate theology: "Who is the image of the invisible God, the firstborn of every creature: for by him were all things created . . . all things were created by him and for him; and he is before all things, and by him all things consist [hang together]" (1:15–17, KJV). The Jesus of history has here become a cosmic quasi-deity; we are in the realm of theological speculation and of myth.

The Cosmic Redeemer

In addition to the Logos-Wisdom line of thought, we must consider one other strand of religious belief that was an important part of the culture of Jesus' time: the myth of the god

who descends to earth, bringing peace, prosperity, and redemption, and then ascends in some miraculous manner. We
have already seen that in Greco-Roman times great poets,
philosophers, and kings were often said to come from divine
parentage and, sometimes, to have been born of virgins. In
the case of Romulus, the legendary founder of Rome, Young
notes that the historian Livy records not only divine conception and a virgin birth, but disappearance of his remains after
death, a return from the dead to commission his followers,
and the offering of prayers to him. She comments that although direct influence is impossible to prove, "people living
at roughly the same time do seem to have produced mythological accounts with parallel motifs."[4] Nowhere is this tendency more apparent than in the mystery religions of the
ancient world, in which converts were initiated into a union
with a dying and rising god and celebrated that union with
various rituals, including a mystical meal. Theologians have
long been aware of the many close resemblances between the
cults of Osiris, Isis, Serapis, Dionysus, and a host of others,
and early Christianity. Charles Talbert cites a number of examples of descent-ascent mythology in which such deities as
Apollo, Jupiter, and Mercury come down to earth in human
guise.[5] That the earliest Christians were aware of these stories
is evident in the Book of Acts, when Paul heals a crippled
man at Lystra: "And when the people saw what Paul had
done, they lifted up their voices, saying ... The gods are
come down to us in the likeness of men. And they called
Barnabas, Jupiter; and Paul, Mercurius, because he was the
chief speaker" (14:8–18; KJV).

But if such thinking was undoubtedly current during the
early formation of Christian belief, many have nevertheless
remained sceptical that the Jewish founders of faith, with
their categorically strict monotheism, could have been influenced directly by these pagan models. As Young points out,
we must remember that it was Paul, a thoroughly Jewish
scholar, who first provided a dogmatic base for the faith that
in Jesus a supernatural agent of God entered the world,
wrought redemption, and then returned to his former glory.[6]
It is highly unlikely Paul would have copied traditions that as
a Jew he would despise. The question is whether similar ideas

were at work in Jewish theology at the time. Had the descending-ascending mythology found its counterpart in Judaism from an earlier date? Talbert presents an overwhelmingly convincing case that it had, establishing not only that a descending-ascending pattern was used for redemption figures in ancient Judaism, but that this Jewish myth served as a model for the way in which some early Christians spoke and taught about Jesus. The following is a very brief outline of his argument.

We have already touched on the Wisdom tradition in Jewish thought. Around the beginning of the Christian era, such literature frequently spoke of the *descent* of Wisdom from heaven to humankind with "saving intent." The Wisdom of Solomon, for example, speaks of a pre-existent Wisdom sent from the heavens as a savior figure for this world and the next; the author actually tells of being "saved by Wisdom." Similarly, these works also speak of the *ascent* of Wisdom to take "her seat among the angels." Thus it is possible to say that the hypostatized Wisdom of late Jewish writing "is an anonymous heavenly redeemer figure" very similar to those in both Greco-Roman and Christian thought. At the same time, Jewish theologizing about angels also made use of the descending-ascending pattern for figures of redemption. In Isaiah 63 it was the "angel of [God's] presence" who "saved" the Israelites—and "in his love and his pity . . . redeemed them." Dozens of similar instances can be found throughout the Old Testament. Talbert also cites numerous instances in extra-biblical writings in which archangels descend in human form. Some of the language used of these angelic redeemers is actually paralleled in the fourth Gospel: in the Testament of Abraham, for example, the archangel comes down and tells the patriarch "everything which he had heard from the Most High," while in another work an archangel, the "firstborn of every creature," descends to earth and "tabernacles" among men. In all these writings there is the taking of bodily form, the successful struggle with evil, and the final ascent of the heavenly being. Moreover, in some cases the angel and Wisdom traditions merge with each other and with the concepts of the Logos and the first-born son. In one of the sources Talbert cites the process is taken further still, and all of these elements merged with the work and activity of the Holy Spirit: "The resulting configuration yields a divine redeemer who is variously identified as Wisdom-Logos-angel-Holy Spirit."[7] This same "many-named one" appears in Philo, where he is sometimes referred to as High-Priest-Man and as the image of God.

Thus Talbert writes that a "myth of a heavenly redeemer who descended and ascended in the course of his/her saving work existed in pre-Christian Judaism and alongside first and second century Christianity."[8] He then goes on to show how Christian authors made use of these concepts both in non-scriptural writings and in the New Testament itself. Certainly parallels with the pattern of pre-existence, descent (redemptive activity), ascent (redemptive activity), and *parousia*, or second coming, are implicit in the writings of St. Paul. No single passage contains all these elements, but the themes of pre-existence, descent, and glorious ascent are found in Philippians 2:6–10, and those of descent and exaltation in Romans 1:3–4, while in Galatians 4:4 there is a clear reference to Christ as an angel: "You received me as an angel of God, even as Christ Jesus." In teaching about Christ as pre-existent, "the image of the invisible God, the firstborn of every creature [by whom] all things were created" (Col. 1:15), clearly Paul is describing not the historical Jesus whose profile we can discern, however dimly, in the Gospels, but with a figure cast in the mold of Wisdom literature speculation—that is, with a mythological construct. The author of the Epistle to the Hebrews, with his own particular aims and audience, patterns his view of Jesus' mission on the same model. The names used for Jesus, as Talbert points out, come straight out of Hellenistic Judaism: Son of God, High Priest, the "character" or stamp of God's nature (a term used by Philo for the Logos), and so on. Hebrews 1:3 speaks of the Son "upholding the universe by the word of his power"—a concept and phraseology also used in Philo's discussion of the Logos.

Finally, many of the philosophical and mythological elements present in the writings of St. Paul and the Epistle to the Hebrews can also be found in the fourth Gospel. Pre-existence is mentioned not only in the Prologue concerning the Word or Logos, but in several other places as well (for example, 1:30, 3:31, and 6:51). Unlike the three earlier Gospels, this one has Jesus speak of himself as descending to earth: "I proceeded from God" (8:42), "I came down from heaven" (6:38), "I am from above" (8:23). His ascent is spoken of in a variety of ways: he was going to God, lifted up, glorified, and so on. This view of Jesus can only be explained in terms of the Jewish Wisdom myth discussed above. And so it is that Talbert reaches his conclusion: "The early Christian myth of a descending-ascending redeemer was taken over from Hellenistic Judaism."[9]

In closing, it is important to stress that this brief look at the roots of the myths that grew up around Jesus in no way clashes with my belief in the actual Resurrection. The fact that God raised him up "on the third day" remains for me the bedrock upon which any meaningful reconstruction of the Christian message must be based. It is one thing to explore the myths; it is another to abandon, in the process, the core truth that gave rise to them.

JESUS FROM NOW ON

A New Reformation

THE PROTESTANT Reformation of the sixteenth century was a major housecleaning for the Christian faith. As the reformers turned more and more to scripture as the basis for belief and action, they discovered that the whole apparatus of a sacrificing priesthood standing between people and God was a "fond thing vainly invented,"[1] and not warranted by the New Testament itself. They rejected the idolatries connected with Transubstantiation and the Mass; they condemned to oblivion the sale of indulgences; and they denied the claims of any one man to be absolute monarch over Christ's Holy Catholic Church. But at the same time the Reformation fathers set the stage for other abuses, which in their own way were to become just as harmful and misleading as the errors they were intended to correct.

The real problem with the Protestant Reformation was that it was not radical enough, not nearly as radical in its purification of religion as Jesus himself was—or aimed to be. In a sense, the reformers were not Protestant enough. I will explain. The essence of the Protestant ethos or spirit is that there is nothing, neither ritual nor priest, standing between the individual and his or her God. There is no "work" required of anyone for God's forgiveness and the gift of eternal life—all is of God's grace, His goodness, bounty, and unconditional gift. Yet what do we find? By putting Jesus, conceived of in the most rigid of God-Man theological terms, between the believer and God, the reformers set the stage for the Jesuolatry of most modern evangelical-style churches—with all of the intolerance and supposed superiority over both other Christians and members of other religions that this nearly always entails. Next to Jesus, and once again blocking the immediacy of direct access to and fellowship with God, they placed the Holy Bible. The infallibility of the pope was replaced by the infallibility of a book—a paper pope reverenced to a degree that can only be described as bibliolatrous.[2]

I have attempted to show that neither of these dogmatic constructs can stand the test of close scrutiny, working with the scriptural evidence itself. What we need desperately today is a new reformation based on the reality of this knowledge. We need to see Jesus afresh, freed of all the dogmatic shackles of the past, freed of the legends and mythologies that worked for other generations but that no longer work for us as we near the year 2000. I believe that if we can see Jesus more nearly as he was, he in turn can help to set us free.

Who Is Jesus Christ for Us Today?

One of the chief preoccupations of the German martyr-theologian Dietrich Bonhoeffer was the shape Christianity would take in the "post-Christian world" following World War II. Bonhoeffer, who was hanged by the Nazis in 1945, used to focus his concern by saying that the most crucial question to face the Church in this new age would be, Who is Jesus Christ for us today? Each word in the query has enormous significance. He was not interested in abstract metaphysical speculations about Jesus' divinity so much as in the practical issue of what he does or means "for us." One of the most exciting things about the Liberation Theology of Latin America and some other developing parts of the world today is that, whatever criticisms the Pope and others may make, it is wrestling with precisely this matter. The Liberation theologians begin with the actual historical and socioeconomic life-setting of the masses of ordinary people in their own countries and ask what the gospel of Jesus means in that context. The "for us" part of Bonhoeffer's question is always at the fore. Coupled with this emphasis is the conviction that any theology of Jesus that is to make sense in the here and now must begin where the gospel story itself begins—with Jesus' humanity, his total identification with all of us, particularly the poor and the oppressed. I am convinced that any attempt to talk meaningfully in North America or anywhere else about "Jesus from now on" must follow these same basic principles.

If it is true that Jesus never went about claiming to be God, that the idea of his being the Second Person of a Holy Trinity is never so much as raised in the New Testament, that even

St. Paul, who saw Christ as pre-existent and the agent of creation, never makes such a claim and is always careful to show Christ as subject to God (see 1 Corinthians 15:28: "And when all things shall be subjected unto him, then shall the Son also himself be subject unto him that put all things under him, that God may be all in all")—if all this is true, a serious question arises. Was Jesus, then, just an extraordinarily gifted preacher and teacher? Was he simply another ethical idealist, only one in a train of prophets who have met their fate at the hands of those not prepared to accept their message? In other words, have we now slipped into what the theologians call "reductionism," the heresy of reducing Jesus to a "mere man"? By no means.

If taking a rational approach to the New Testament means we have to peel away—or see in a new, symbolic light—the dogmatic additions and exaggerations formulated in the fourth and fifth centuries, it also poses another question. What was it about Jesus of Nazareth that so impressed his early followers that they used all the exalted titles they could think of to describe him? What was it that led them to the deep conviction that God was acting uniquely in him to bring "salvation" to all humanity, that to see him clearly was to see God? Failure to answer this question adequately leaves us with an enormous difficulty: the whole movement known as Christianity, surely one of the most influential forces in human history (if not *the* most), becomes inexplicable, an effect totally lacking a sufficient cause to explain it.

Jesus' Claims to Authority

Even in the earliest strata of the tradition, the Gospels make it evident that Jesus surprised his contemporaries first and foremost by the strange note of authority in his teaching and preaching. As early as Chapter 1 of Mark it is stated that his observers "were all amazed, insomuch that they questioned among themselves, saying, What thing is this? what new doctrine is this? for with authority commandeth he even the unclean spirits, and they do obey him" (v. 27, KJV). In Chapter 6, when Jesus is preaching in the synagogue, we read that "many, hearing him, were astonished, saying, From whence hath this man these things? and what wisdom is this which is given unto him . . . ?" (v. 2). It was said of Jesus that he taught with authority "and not as the scribes." All his hearers were familiar with the way the scribes tried to interpret the Mosaic law in contemporary terms. What was strikingly different with Jesus was the manner in which he was accustomed to speak: "Moses said unto you . . . but I say unto you . . ." It was the expression "but I say" that so startled everyone. Thus in Mark 11 we find the chief priests, the scribes, and the elders in Jerusalem challenging him pointedly: "By what authority doest thou these things? and who gave thee this authority to do these things?" (v. 28). Significantly, Jesus refuses to answer their question and instead traps them with a question of his own about the authority of John the Baptist. Implicit in this silence is the certainty that the source of his authority will be recognized by those with the eyes to see and ears to hear. His appeal is not to an external source of authority but to the "voice of conscience within," the still, small voice of God.

With a daring—given the veneration for the words of Moses in his day—that was literally astounding, Jesus did not so much abrogate or attempt to abolish the central teachings of his own Jewish heritage as to radicalize them: he went back beyond the letter of the law to the deeper spiritual truth behind it. Murder is thus not just a matter of physically killing someone; it is first of all an act of hatred in the heart. External rituals, cleansings, and ceremonies of purification are meaningless without the inner purity of heart and conscience they are meant to symbolize. Jesus saw that the Sabbath's meaning was being perverted in the anxiety to safeguard it by excessive rules and regulations. Like the Old Testament prophets, he denounced the entire attempt to win God's favor and forgiveness through observance of the trappings of religion. His concern was with what was going on in people's hearts and with the issuance of this genuine spirituality in the "fruits" of concrete actions on behalf of the needy and the marginalized in society. His authority in taking on the whole religious establishment of his day—and so all subsequent establishments that claim his name—came from the clarity of his own moral vision, the certainty that his heavenly Father wanted "mercy and not sacrifice" (Hosea 6:6) from those seeking His Kingdom.

We have said earlier that Jesus was a prophet like Amos or Isaiah. He called himself a prophet and his contemporaries gave him the same title. Yet the prophets always spoke in the name of God or Yahweh. Jesus is a new kind of prophet who speaks in his own name. As Edward Schillebeeckx has written: "He radicalized the Torah and did so on his own authority. And that is something I have not been able to find anywhere in the Old Testament."[3] The renowned theologian points out that although Jesus was in the classical prophetic tradition, he also saw himself as "more than a prophet." "It is part of his consciousness of himself. He is the 'eschatological' prophet, the ultimate prophet proclaiming the gospel to the poor."[4] It was this uniqueness, this going beyond anything hitherto claimed by other prophets, that helped to impress on his followers that in him God was saying something and doing something more final than ever before. Their experience of the Resurrection confirmed this faith—or, rather, made it all glow with transcendent meaning.

Jesus and the Kingdom of God

I was brought up in a very traditionally evangelical home— and I will always be grateful for all it taught me. However, part of that tradition was the orthodox view that the central message of Christianity is Jesus himself. It came as a great shock to me later, when studying the Bible for myself, to discover that this is not what the Gospels say at all. Jesus did not come proclaiming himself; he came proclaiming the good news of God's Kingdom. For Schillebeeckx, what the Kingdom expresses is the fact that "God's affair is man's affair. God identifies with man's affair. He is concerned with oppressed and enslaved men."[5] Against all appearances to the contrary, Jesus boldly affirms that God is in control not just of the universe of nature but of human destiny. His Kingdom is near, in our midst, and can be entered into now. It is present or made visible wherever right relationships are being established, wherever justice and mercy are being shown. It is not something you gain membership in because you belong to a special social, racial, sexual, or other group. It is a free gift to all who have the simplicity and the sincerity of spirit to receive it. It is a fellowship of all those who are forgiving because they themselves have first become aware of how freely they have been forgiven. This forgiveness depends not on priests or other hierarchies acting as mediators. It has been pronounced by Jesus as free and available to any who seek or ask for it. It does not depend on blood sacrifice. It is already there because it is the very nature of God to be forgiving to all who call upon Him. He is the Lord who "forgiveth all thine iniquities; who healeth all thy diseases" (Psalm 103:3, KJV). Jesus was able to say authoritatively that in his presence the Kingdom of God "has come nigh" because he was aware that God had chosen him to proclaim this message and that God's Holy Spirit was moving in him, confirming this message in power. The miracles of healing were signs of this reality.

My second surprise in reading the New Testament for myself was that, contrary to what most churches teach, Jesus' principle concern was not with sin but with humanity's real enemy: fear. His vision of God as reigning meant that he could relax from all anxiety and fear. Jesus called on people to have faith; not faith in creeds or dogmas or traditions or organizations, but faith—that is, radical trust—in God. The message that God is in ultimate control and that He seeks our cooperation in realizing His Kingdom "on earth as it is in heaven" is good news. It is particularly good news when coupled with the message that we can cast aside our fears and accept or enter this Kingdom through childlike trust.

But one other thing is still lacking. What kind of God is in control? What guarantee have we that He is not some sadistic monster bent on torturing us for our own supposed good— or for no reason at all? This is where Jesus and his message become absolutely central. No matter how critical our approach to the New Testament evidence may be, we are brought face to face with the certainty of the part of its authors that in Jesus Christ we have, as it were, a window into the heart of the living God. Through his parables and sayings, and then through the "acted parable" of his own life and crucifixion, Jesus taught that the Creator and Sustainer of the cosmos says "yes" to humanity, a "yes" of wholly unconditional love, forgiveness, and acceptance. While priestly and other forms of religion stressed the external duties and rituals required for any reconciliation with God, the Ground of our being, the "depth dimension" of all that is truly human, Jesus showed—for example, in the parables of the prodigal son and of the lost coin—that God Himself is already offering freely this wholeness or salvation. His Kingdom is already present within us, among us. We can cease our frantic striving and relax as we accept the truth that we have been accepted, and secure in this experience, we can go out empowered by His Spirit to accept others.

In speaking to us through Jesus, God has used the most potent medium of communication known to us as human beings: another human personality. The earliest disciples, with all their faults and frailties, were convinced that in the words and life of Jesus they had come to an encounter with "the words of eternal life," that through him they were being directly addressed by God. Henceforth they worshipped in his name and prayed not to him, but in his name. That is, from then on they knew they were in relationship with a "Jesus-like" God. They worshipped and prayed in the light of and in keeping with the character of Jesus' revelation of the Father. Those who are faithful to his name today will do the same.

Was Jesus Unique?

A lot of Christian talk about the uniqueness of Jesus verges on nonsense because it seems to assume an *absolute uniqueness*. As Stewart R. Sutherland points out, the uniqueness of *absolute* difference postulates a being about whom we can say nothing at all.[6] If someone or something is absolutely different, then there is no point of contact, no meaningful terms that can be applied to him, her, or it. If Jesus is unique, it must be a relative uniqueness with respect to some feature or aspect of his life and teaching. Thus if Jesus was, as I have argued, fully human and not some sort of God-in-disguise, in what did his uniqueness, his difference from other teachers and from us, lie? I have already described his authority and his remarkable certainty, in the face of all appearances, in the ultimate victory of love and justice—a faith that God vindicated by raising him from the dead. He was different from us not because of some metaphysical or ontological difference—some difference of essence or being—but in the degree to which he was obedient to the God he knew as Father and the extent to which he opened himself to the presence and guidance of God's Breath (*pneuma*) or Spirit within.

The pages of the New Testament itself give us a number of clear indications that this is how some at least of the Apostles and their successors understood the nature and dynamic of their Master. Luke, who has the greatest interest in the experience of God's nearness to and indwelling in humans by His Holy Spirit, clearly understands the sonship of Jesus in this pneumatic way. The passage that is crucial for Lucan theology—and which has become so pivotal for Liberation Theology today—is in Luke 4:1ff.: "And Jesus being full of the Holy Spirit, returned from Jordan, and was led by the Spirit into the wilderness. . . ." That this was how Jesus understood himself and his entire ministry becomes clear when he reads from the prophet Isaiah—"The spirit of the Lord is upon me . . ."—and announced himself to be the anointed one come to make known God's will for the liberation of all who suffer from injustice and evil. I believe that if the theologians of the fourth and fifth centuries had followed this Spirit-filled Jewish line of reasoning instead of splitting philosophical and theological hairs in the manner of the Greek academies—arguing over whether Jesus was *homoousios* (of the same nature) or *homoiousios* (of a similar nature) with the Father, a difference of one letter!—the Church would have been spared the terrible damage that resulted from making Jesus into God.

What needs to be said in any attempt to understand and follow Jesus *from now on* is that his uniqueness consisted not in having two natures, one divine and one human, but in having exactly the same human nature we all possess, but wholly filled with God's Spirit and obedience to His will. It is a difference that can be measured qualitatively, not some mystical difference in kind. We are all, as the Bible repeatedly makes clear, to be fully the sons or children of God. Even

John's Gospel, with its exalted view of Jesus, says that all who believe in him (accept his message) are given the "power to become the sons of God." Jesus was the Son of God precisely to the degree that he was open to and obedient to the source of his and our own being. He called, and still calls, on all of us to be such ourselves. He was not more "divine" than we are but more *human,* in the sense that the Bible teaches throughout that God created us for this close relationship with Himself. Human nature is most truly human when it is in touch with and rooted in the spiritual, in the cosmic mind and energy we call God. As the letter to the Hebrews says, Jesus was our forerunner or "pioneer" in exploring and making this territory known (6:20).

Summary

We understand best who Jesus is for our time and for the future if we see him as God's agent of hope and salvation, as the one who is to be obeyed as master—or even, if you prefer, as guru—rather than worshipped idolatrously as God.[7] It has always been much easier for Christians to worship Jesus as "King of kings and Lord of lords" than to do the will of the Father as he commanded. In spite of the fact that he himself warned against those who go around saying "Lord, Lord" and at the same time perpetuating intolerance, religious elitism, even war, traditional orthodoxy has at one time or another justified every possible kind of crime against humanity. The missionary history of the Church is replete with horrific acts of intolerance against those who confess not Jesus but some other proclaimer of the way to the Ground of all being, while as we have already seen, even Martin Luther was capable of vitriolic attacks on the Jewish people. Indeed, it is very doubtful whether the Holocaust of the Jews under Hitler could ever have taken place had it not been for centuries of hostility toward them based on the blasphemous allegation that they were "Christ-killers"—the murderers of God Incarnate.

Unless it begins to take Jesus *seriously* as its master and guide, the Christian Church will continue to be part of the world's problems, its dangerous tensions, its propensity for war. That is why the growing intolerance in the United States

on the part of Fundamentalists toward those of differing
moral and religious views—the attacks on pluralism and liberal humanism—is so dismaying. You cannot profess to follow
Jesus and yet approve of violence, nuclear or other. You cannot follow him and insist that your vision of God is the only
one, that your group has cornered the market on divine
truth. You cannot proclaim him as your Lord and ignore
everything he said about limitless forgiveness, about loving
your neighbor, about loving your enemies. You cannot permit
patriotism and the lust for power to supersede the urgent
command to "seek first the Kingdom of God." You cannot
partake of his meal of remembrance, the Holy Communion,
and not be part of the quest for an end to all injustice, poverty,
and misery for all peoples everywhere. For too long the
churches have tried to spiritualize Jesus' statement, "I am
come that they might have life, and have it more abundantly"
(John 10:10). Clearly, what he was talking about was not some
pie in the sky, but a full life of right-relatedness in the here
and now.

There is not a shred of evidence in the New Testament that
Jesus ever intended to found an institution such as the highly
structured, terribly divided Christian Church has become. He
was out to reform the Judaism of his day by radically re-
focusing its life and vision on the living God. He remained a
pious Jew throughout his life, always worshipping either in
the synagogues or in the Temple in Jerusalem. The earliest
Christians continued to worship in the same manner—even
St. Paul always went to the synagogue first on his great missionary journeys—until they were thrown out and persecuted
for proclaiming one who had died scandalously on a cross.
Jesus said nothing about bishops, priests, deacons, elders, or
any other church functionary of the present. He said nothing
about a pope; in fact, he was pointedly against the notion of
calling any man "father"—which is what "pope" means. He
said nothing either about magnificent church buildings, cathedrals, or elaborate rituals of worship. The first Christians
worshipped in people's homes or out of doors when the synagogues became closed to them. Because he knew that the
same Spirit of God that had guided his ministry would be
present with them, and because he was deeply aware of the

essential solidarity of all human beings with each other, he was able to promise that wherever even two or three were gathered together in his name—that is, in the light of the revelation of God he had proclaimed—he would also be "in their midst."

This is by no means to say that faithfulness to Jesus from now on will mean abandoning institutional religion, destroying its buildings, and ignoring its rituals. It means rather re-forming and renewing every aspect of this cultus so that it truly embodies the teaching he has given. Instead of focusing on the messenger, life and worship must radiate with the message. There is an urgent need to look where Jesus was pointing, to hear what he was proclaiming, to come to genuine encounter with the God Whose witness he was. Once that begins to happen, the ideal of reaching out to embrace not only other Christians but also those of all the other great world religions—and of none—will transcend the ecumenical rhetoric and double-speak we have now to become a reality.

Myths, those great truths that can only be communicated by means of stories, function at many different levels as they assist us to place ourselves in relation to God, self, others, and the universe as a whole. To take the myths of orthodox Christian theology literally is not only to make a fundamental error about the nature and purpose of the mythical, but to disregard Jesus' command to love God with all one's *mind*, because they plainly cannot be sustained as historical. But that does not mean we have to abandon them entirely. At one very deep level, the myth of God-in-human-form, the myth of the Christ of faith rather than the Jesus of history, speaks a truth that is one of the oldest and most universal religious ideas known to humanity. That is the insight or belief that each one of us comes from God and lives, moves, and has his or her being in God; that each of us has a measure of His Spirit, an inner divinity, as an essential part of ourselves, and that we will one day be raised up beyond death to an eternal destiny with Him. At the unconscious level where all myths find their origin, the evangelists and early Christians saw in Jesus the prototype or "pioneer" of our common calling and our eventual future. There are many clues to this reality in the Gospels and other New Testament writings, but to find them we have to drop the obsession with literal truth and begin to look for the meaning behind the symbolism and imagery.

For example, look at the Prologue to John's Gospel, where Jesus is said to be the Logos, God's Word, by which He created all things: "the true light that lighteth every person coming into the world [*cosmos*]." The Greek is ambiguous in that it can mean "that lighteth every person as *it* [the light] comes into the world," or, "that lighteth every person as *he/she* comes into the world." But the overall thrust is much the same. What is being so sublimely stated is that all of us—you and I and every other person ever to walk the face of the earth—have within us a spark or "seed" (to use the Stoic concept) of divine light that is none other than God. As Paul says, quoting pagan poets, "In him we live and move and have our being" (Acts 17:28). When Jesus says that the Kingdom of God is "within you," he is speaking of the same thing. In a sense, the whole summons of Jesus on God's behalf is this: become what you are; realize your God-given potential; take power *to be the son or daughter of God you already are*. When he calls us to encounter God in his message and ministry, it is not a call to worship some remote first cause, far away in the skies, but to find anew God's gift of Himself within. Our true humanity lies, paradoxically, in our divinity.

Thus it would be wrong to conclude from this book that I, and those who think as I do, no longer believe in the divinity of Jesus Christ. I believe very strongly in his divinity in the sense that God was indeed working mightily in and through him. But I also believe in the divinity within and at the core of every human being. Jesus, to use the terminology of Eastern mysticism, was certainly "more fully realized" as a person than you or I. He had traveled much further along the path of allowing the presence of God within to control and direct his life—"he had learned obedience through suffering," to quote Hebrews (5:8). He was open to God and open to his fellows, especially the weak, the hungry and the outcast, to a degree far beyond that of anyone before or since. If you like, he had already made that spiritual "quantum leap" that we now realize all humanity must begin to make if our broken, endangered world is to survive. He was not just what the theologians of the sixties called "the man for others"—he was, and remains, "the man for the future" (or rather the human being for the future) as well.

I have no objection to reciting the ancient creeds or preserving much of the symbolic language of orthodoxy. The point is simply to remember that—as with all language about God—it is *symbolic*. Schillebeeckx has written that the old Nicene creed should be retained as a "shared sign of recognition" for all Christians.[8] I agree. And I also share his view that, in the light of our new understanding of Jesus and the Gospels, we have a duty to attempt to formulate new creeds to explain our faith in Jesus from now on—creeds that as far as possible speak to modern men and women and avoid unnecessary mental obstacles for the "outsider" of goodwill. "I think it is quite right to formulate modern creeds—if we Christians have any real self-respect, we are bound in the long run to do that."[9] With these words in mind, I would like to conclude with a personal statement of how I think such a modern creed might read.

A New Creed for a Church Nearing the Year of Our Lord 2000

We believe and put our unconditional trust in God, Creator and Sustainer of all things, from the farthest-flung galaxies to the most microscopic forms of life; "He" is above and around and within everyone of us, and yet so far beyond us in glory that our minds cannot fathom the mystery, and our only response is to bow in worship and in wonder. And we believe God sent Jesus, anointing him in the power of "His" Spirit, to declare by word and deed the gospel of personal and social liberation from the power of fear and all injustice and oppression. Though he was cruelly and unjustly put to death on a cross, God raised him from the grave and set "His" seal forever on his message and his ministry. In him we know that God is love, and that forgiveness and acceptance are ours today and every day. In him we are called to realize God's Kingdom in our own lives and in the lives of others, particularly the poor and needy. In him we are called to join with our heavenly Parent in making all things new. We believe God grants to us the same Holy Spirit that was in Jesus, creating community and empowering us to be "His" sons and daughters. We believe in a life and a dimension of existence yet to come on the other side of death. We seek to build God's Kingdom here, but we also look beyond to that day when wars shall be no more and God's New Jerusalem shall be revealed. We believe. This is our faith. God help our unbelief. For Christ's sake, Amen.

Holy Week, 1985

Conclusion

I am well aware that in questioning orthodox teaching—the dogmas of the Trinity and the Godhead of Jesus, the divine origins of priestly castes, the necessity of a pyramid-shaped hierarchy, the theory of Atonement, the infallibility of the New Testament documents, and Christianity's absolutist claim to be the only true way to God—I may be denounced as heretical. I can only point out that it is impossible to "prove" from the Bible that Jesus Christ was committed to any such doctrines himself; nor did the earliest disciples hold them all to be true. To state it bluntly, if these creedal tenets are considered the sole criteria, then, as I said at the outset, Jesus was not a Christian. It is obvious from our sources that—insofar as we can talk about his religion—Jesus remained a practising Jew all his days; he was a devout "son of the covenant." The religion *about* Jesus, which developed later, was what became orthodox Christianity. It is my conviction that this development ended in a serious distortion of who he was and what he came to do.

The earliest Christians, scholars agree, confessed but one simple creed: Jesus is Lord (or Jesus Christ is Lord). This did not mean "Jesus is God"—they knew better—but "Jesus is master of my life; I owe my obedience to his teaching about God, his example, his way." That is precisely what being a Christian means to me. So I cling to my membership within the Christian fold, whatever some may say. As Jesus once taught, we must not judge others lest we ourselves be judged. This kind of discipleship judges none to be heretics, none to be outside God's plan of wholeness or "salvation" for humanity. It lies wholly open to the vision of God's truth in all the world's great religions and to His "light" in the life of every person. It stands firmly on the saying of Jesus that belonging to the Kingdom is not a matter of piously using the "right" words or rituals, but of humbly seeking to do the will of God.

The torments and divisions the world suffers today are in scandalous measure the result, however unwitting, of the intolerance and self-righteousness of man-made orthodox Christian positions. This book is a plea to let these go, to hear him, and to follow him afresh in that "newness of life" which is always wrought by love—for Christ's sake.

Jesus said: "This is my commandment, that you love one another, as I have loved you. Greater love has no man [person] than this, that one lay down his life for his friends. You are my friends, if you keep my commandments" (John 15:12–14).

NOTES

PROLOGUE

1. Sydney Carter, *Love More or Less* (Claremont, Cal.: Galliard Press, 1971).

2. I owe the inspiration for this story to Rev. Herbert O'Driscoll, former dean of Vancouver's Christ Church Cathedral, who attributes it to Ira Progoff, *The Well and the Cathedral;* however, I must take responsibility for this version.

THE PROBLEM

1. See *Harpur's Heaven and Hell* (Toronto: Oxford Univ. Press, 1983), 10–11. (Hereafter cited as *Heaven and Hell.*)

2. See Reginald Bibby, "The Circulation of the Saints," *Journal for the Scientific Study of Religion,* Sept. 1973; and his updated report "The Circulation of the Saints Revisited," *ibid.,* Sept. 1983.

3. This creed, widely used today in the Anglican and other churches, is first found *ca.* A.D. 390. It is certainly not of Apostolic origin. See F.L. Cross and E.A. Livingstone, eds., *The Oxford Dictionary of the Christian Church,* 2d ed. (Oxford: Oxford Univ. Press, 1974 [reprinted 1977]), 75.

4. See *Heaven and Hell,* 19.

5. Don Cupitt, "The Christ of Christendom," in John Hick, ed., *The Myth of God Incarnate* (London: SCM Press, 1977), 140–1.

6. See "Chalcedon, definition of," in *Dictionary of the Christian Church,* 263.

7. Quoted in H.G. Haile, *Luther* (New York: Doubleday, 1980), 287ff.

8. In the fourth century John Chrysostom, the great preacher of Constantinople, said in a sermon, "The synagogue is a place of prostitution . . . a den of thieves and a hiding place of wild animals." See Rev. Victor Shepherd, "Holocaust Seeds in Christianity," *United Church Observer,* June 1985, 43ff., and A. Roy Eckardt, *Long Night's Journey Into Day* (Cleveland: Wayne State Univ. Press, 1982), *passim.*

9. Rev. David Lochead, address to the Naramata Interfaith Consultation, June 1983.

10. For an inside look at the Born Again movement in Canada and the U.S., see Judith Haiven, *Faith, Hope—No Charity* (Vancouver:

New Star Books, 1984). Haiven documents the intolerance of fundamentalists towards all others: ". . . beyond the initial friendliness there is a barrier as hard as steel to those not of their thinking . . . a 'we versus them' mentality . . . they are holy warriors locked in a deadly battle" (p. 16).

11. In Cardinal G. Emmett Carter's Pastoral Letter of Dec. 8, 1983 (published by the Archdiocese of Toronto), he argues that restriction of the priesthood to males is rooted in the doctrine of the Trinity: "The qualitative differentiation of men and women is . . . sacramental and liturgical. It is integral to the Good Creation, to the Covenant, to the worship by which the Church is constituted as the Body, the Bride of Christ. This qualitative sexual differentiation is rooted not in physiology but in the created human imaging of the Trinity in Christ, as his Incarnation bears witness" (p. 41). The language of this document is so convoluted—e.g., "The application of sexual symbolism, of sexual sacramentality, to the understanding of priestly orders is intrinsic to the sacrament" (p. 52)—and filled with theological jargon that even the priests of the diocese found it difficult, but it is worth reading for anyone who needs further proof that Christ's maleness has profoundly shaped Trinitarian thinking.

12. *Heaven and Hell,* 137ff.

THE STRANGER FROM GALILEE

1. "New Testament scholarship today agrees Jesus of Nazareth was baptized by John the Baptist, that as a teacher and healer Jesus attracted disciples, and that he was executed by crucifixion. Biblical research has made anything else historically questionable." (Prof. Van Harvey, chairman of Stanford University's Religious Studies Department, quoted in the *Toronto Star,* May 18, 1985.)

2. The name is derived from Yeshua (Joshua) and means "deliverer."

3. Unless otherwise noted, Biblical translations are my own.

4. The Book of Acts tells us they were first called "Christianoi"—people who follow Christ—in the city of Antioch.

THE MESSAGE

1. There are many technical reasons for the belief that Mark's is the first Gospel. Here I will only outline the essentials. Like the earliest preaching recorded in Acts 1:22ff., Mark includes no birth narrative, few parables, and no Sermon on the Mount (Matthew) or Sermon on the Plain (Luke). In other words, its limited scope suggests that it is primitive material. So too does the fact that Mark

records certain (perhaps embarrassing) details that Matthew and Luke either soften or omit altogether; see, for example, Mark's frequent references to the disciples' inability to understand what was happening (4:13, 6:52, 8:17ff., 9:10, 32, 34, etc.) and his statement in 3:21 (omitted by the other two) that Jesus' relatives once came to take him in hand forcibly because, they said, "he is beside himself," i.e., crazy or mad. The language in Mark also provides evidence of Aramaic origins (Aramaic was the language of Palestine in Jesus' time), suggesting an early Palestinian source or sources. Papias, Bishop of Hieropolis in Asia Minor *ca.* A.D. 125, records the tradition that Mark owed most of what he wrote to the Apostle Peter: "Mark, having become the interpreter of Peter, wrote down accurately everything that he remembered, without, however, recording in order what was either said or done by Christ. For neither did he hear the Lord, nor did he follow him; but, afterwards . . . attended Peter who *adapted his instructions to the needs of his hearers* but had no design of giving a connected account of the Lord's oracles" (cited in A.S. Peake, *A Commentary on the Bible*, 2d ed. with supplement [London: Nelson, 1937], 681; my italics). Papias, who goes on to protest rather too much about Mark's accuracy, tells us a good deal here. In addition to stating that Mark did not know Jesus personally, he admits what any reader must notice—that Mark has virtually no chronology, but rather a string of anecdotes loosely connected by such phrases as "immediately then," or "and it came to pass that." What is more, he says Peter adapted his preaching and use of Jesus' words and deeds to the needs of his hearers; in other words, what Mark gives us is simply what he remembers of material already reshaped by Peter. Translate this account into Greek and then into English, and you are at least three or four stages away from the facts (Jesus himself, remember, would have spoken Aramaic).

   2. Anyone wishing to explore in detail what is known as the Synoptic problem—the relations between the first three Gospels—may consult the Readings below, pp. 113–14. In brief, it should be noted that scholars are fairly unanimous in their view that both Matthew and Luke had Mark's account before them as they wrote and that, between them, they used most of the Marcan material. In addition, however, both made use of a common written source consisting of sayings of Jesus; this is usually refered to as "Q" (from the German *Quelle,* source). Besides "Q," both Matthew and Luke are assumed to have their own particular sources, since each includes some material that the other does not—see, for example, the differences in their accounts of the Resurrection. These two sources are known technically as "M" and "L." Thus Matthew is made up of Mark (modified) plus "Q" plus "M"; Luke is composed of Mark plus "Q" plus "L."

Fundamentalists who insist that every word in the Bible is the literally inspired Word of God do not know what to make of the fact that neither Matthew nor Luke viewed Mark's account in this unrealistic way. They used his material, but felt no taboo whatever against changing or omitting anything of which they either disapproved or felt no need.

3. See John Macmurray, *To Save from Fear* (London: Friends House, July 1964), 4. This monograph was first presented as four talks on the B.B.C., Lent 1964.

4. *Ibid.*

5. See Henry Drummond, *The Greatest Thing in the World* (Old Tappan, N.J.: Fleming H. Revell, 1981 [15th printing]). For a contemporary presentation of the same idea, see Gerald G. Jampolsky, *Love Is Letting Go of Fear* (New York: Bantam, 1981).

THE MYTH OF THE VIRGIN BIRTH

1. See *Heaven and Hell,* 20.

2. Some scholars believe that the "Ministry of the Word" (Acts 6:4) to which the Twelve devoted themselves refers in part to the study of the Old Testament.

3. F.W. Beare, *The Gospel According to Matthew* (New York: Harper and Row, 1981), 72.

4. *Ibid.,* 75.

5. Example cited by Frances Young, "Two Roots or a Tangled Mass?" in *Myth of God Incarnate,* 89.

6. See *Heaven and Hell,* 12.

7. See J.N.D. Kelly, *Early Christian Doctrines* rev. ed. (New York: Harper and Row, 1960), 490ff.

8. *Ibid.,* 498.

9. See John Dourley, *The Illness That We Are: A Jungian Critique of Christianity* (Toronto: Inner City Books, 1984).

THE HUMANITY OF JESUS

1. See Ernest W. Harrison, *Church without God* (Toronto: McClelland and Stewart, 1966).

THE TEACHINGS OF JESUS

1. In the first half of the third century, Origen urged that prayer be made through the Son to the Father alone.

2. The words "For thine is the kingdom, the power and the glory,

forever and ever, Amen" are not found in the earliest manuscripts, but were added by a later hand.

3. Introduced by Paul Tillich and popularized by John Robinson in *Honest to God* (London: SCM Press, 1963), this phrase avoids many of the misconceptions associated with the traditional idea of God as being "up there" or "out there" somewhere; it states the reality that He is at the center of our existence.

4. *Heaven and Hell*, 9.

5. On May 9, 1985, the Vatican's powerful Congregation for the Doctrine of the Faith, the modern successor to the Inquisition, ordered a year of silence—no sermons, articles, or books—for Fr. Leonardo Boff, the prominent Brazilian Liberation theologian who has questioned Church authority in his book *Church: Charism and Power* (New York: Crossroads, 1985). Fr. Edward Schillebeeckx, the leading theologian in the Netherlands, has also been disciplined for his writings on Jesus and his challenges to the Church's hierarchical structures. On May 8, 1985, the eve of the Pope's visit to the Netherlands, Schillebeeckx told a rally in Holland that the hierarchical structure of the Church "was not willed by God" but was the result of developments in the sixteenth century, and added that personifying infallibility in the pope "is from the Roman Catholic point of view a clear heresy." World-renowned Catholic theologian Hans Küng has been stripped of his right to that title because of his book *Infallible? An Inquiry* (New York: Doubleday, 1971), in which he too disputes this doctrine. These extreme measures indicate the determination of Church authorities to check any erosion of priestly and papal power in favor of the laity. (See *Catholic New Times*, vol. 9, no. 10 [June 2, 1985].)

6. L.S. Greenslade, *Schisms in the Early Church* (London: SCM Press, 1953), 15.

7. *Ibid.*, 15–16 (my italics).

JESUS AS PROPHET

1. See, for example, Jean Tillard, *The Bishop of Rome*, Theology and Life Series, vol. 5 (Wilmington, Del.: Michael Glazier, 1983).

THE FOURTH GOSPEL

1. As I write this, Pope John Paul II is on a tour of Latin America. According to a Reuter news report, he has told crowds of the faithful in Merida, Venezuela, that as good Catholics they must never question any teaching of the Church; being faithful to the gospel means "accepting with docility the magisterium [teaching authority] and

making its teachings known" (*Toronto Star*, January 29, 1985). This statement seems strangely inconsistent with Jesus' command to love God with all one's mind, and with the *Book of Common Prayer's* insistence on a "reasonable hope" (*BCP Canada* [1959], 599). The truth is that the Pope is afraid that if the faithful begin to ask questions, the whole edifice will collapse; this is an attitude widely shared in other churches as well.

THE ACTS OF THE APOSTLES

1. Arianism, the most serious of all the "heresies" that plagued the Church in the third, fourth, and fifth centuries, takes its name from Arius, a brilliant Bible scholar and priest of Alexandira. Born in Libya *ca.* A.D. 250 (died 336 in Constantinople), Arius became convinced that the New Testament clearly teaches Jesus' subordination to God the Father. He said that the Son of God was not eternal, but was created by the Father as His instrument for creating the world. Jesus was thus not God by nature or essence, but was given his high rank because he found favor with God through his obedience. Arius' views were bitterly attacked, and he was excommunicated by a Church council of all Egypt in 318. However, he found powerful support from a number of bishops elsewhere, particularly Eusebius of Caesarea (the "Father of Church History") and Eusebius of Nicomedia. Their advocacy of his views spread the debate from Egypt throughout the Eastern Church. Constantine I, who conquered the East in 324 and wanted unity in the Empire before all else, wrote to Arius and his chief opponent, Alexander, Bishop of Alexandria, asking them to stop fighting over what to him seemed "a trifling and foolish verbal difference." This was a reference to the fact that the two parties each had a word to describe Christ's relationship to the Godhead. They differed by one letter, the Greek *iota:* Arius said Jesus was *homoiousios,* "of a like or similar substance to God", and thus not identical with Him; Alexander and the rest insisted Jesus was *homoousios,* "of the very same substance" as the Father.

The Emperor's pleas fell on deaf ears, and in 325 he called together the famous council of the whole Church, the Council of Nicaea, to settle the dispute. Largely through the efforts of Athanasius, Arius was defeated as the assembly voted for the *homoousios* doctrine of co-equality, co-eternity, and consubstantiality of the Son with the Father. The Arians were banished for a time, but the debate was far from over. In 335 the Assembly of Jerusalem readmitted Arius to the Church (he died on the eve of his official reinstatement) and in 337 Constantine himself, who had always leaned towards the Arian position, recalled all the banished bishops. His successor Constantius openly supported the doctrine, and after a series of councils in the East accepted various shades of Arianism as well, in 359 a double council of East and West accepted an Arian definition for the entire Church; however, the victory was short-lived. Orthodoxy finally triumphed in 381 at the Council of Constantinople. See *Oxford Dictionary of the Christian Church*, 83.

2. See II Cor. 5:16: ". . . yea, though we have known Christ after the flesh, yet now henceforth we know him no more" (KJV).

THE MIRACLES OF JESUS

1. See Mark 8:11, Luke 11:29, and Matthew 12:38: "Teacher, we want to see a sign from you."

2. Humphrey Carpenter, *Jesus* (Oxford: Oxford Univ. Press, 1980), 73–4.

3. Beare, *Gospel According to Matthew*, 258.

4. Carpenter, *Jesus*, 73.

THE TITLES OF JESUS

1. Compare Job 38:7: "and all the sons of God shouted for joy."

2. See above, p. 00.

3. For a full discussion of the title Son of God in Judaism at the time of Jesus, see Young in *Myth of God Incarnate*, 104–17: "In general it can be said that for Jews a son of God was a being of god-like qualities or one specially called and designated by God for a particular task" (p. 105).

4. The only other reference in the New Testament is in Acts 7:56.

5. Barnabas Lindars, *Jesus Son of Man* (Grand Rapids, Mich.: Eerdmans, 1984), 31.

6. *Ibid.*, 188.

7. Lindars concludes that the "Son of Man, as *traditionally* understood, belongs to the development of Christology which took place in the burst of creativity which accompanied the emergence of Christianity in the post-resurrection period. But the Son of Man starts simply as an idiomatic feature of Jesus' speech" (*ibid.*, 189 [my italics]).

THE DEATH OF JESUS

1. Some of the early Fathers, including Origen and St. Gregory of Nyssa, believed that the devil held over fallen humanity certain rights that it was a leading purpose of the cross to satisfy. St. Anselm (*ca.* 1033–1109), Archbishop of Canterbury, strongly repudiated this

view in his work *Cur Deus Homo*, interpreting Jesus' death as the satisfaction due the outraged majesty of a holy God.

2. Among the many parallels in the ancient world was the myth of Osiris, the basis for the Egyptian doctrine of eternal life and the resurrection of a transformed body. After a cruel death inflicted by the powers of darkness and evil, Osiris conquered over all and was taken into glory. According to the Book of the Dead, he came to be known as "king of eternity," "firstborn son of the womb of Nut, the god of gods, the lord of lords, the giver of life from the beginning. Life . . . springs up to us from his destruction" (A.E. Wallis Budge, ed. *The Book of the Dead: The Papyrus of Ani* [reprint; New York: Dover, 1967], liii). (The papyrus acquired by the British Museum dates from between 1500 and 1400 B.C.).

3. Compare Psalm 130: "There is forgiveness with thee . . . for with the Lord there is mercy and . . . plenteous redemption (KJV).

4. See *Heaven and Hell*, 6–7.

5. For a modern psychiatrist's view of how the symbolism of the cross can be therapeutic in one's own life, see James Wilkes, *The Gift of Courage* (Toronto: Anglican Book Centre, 1979).

THE RESURRECTION OF JESUS

1. See *Heaven and Hell*, 93–5 and 242–3 and my article "Resurrection: What the Disciples Saw," *United Church Observer*, May 1984.

2. While the four Gospels vary widely in their accounts of Jesus' Resurrection—on the number of angels at the grave, the exact place where the Risen Lord first met with his disciples, etc.—they agree that the tomb was found empty. Much has been made of this fact by modern Christian apologists, especially among conservatives, but for most scholars the question remains open. What is most significant is that, as far as we can tell, the teaching about the empty tomb played no part in early Apostolic preaching. St. Paul, whose writings make up at least a third of the whole New Testament, never mentions the empty tomb; nor does the Book of Acts in its reports of the earliest Apostolic sermons. For Paul, what counted as evidence of the Resurrection were the appearances of the Risen Lord, while even in the Gospels it was not the tomb which produced faith that Jesus had been raised up—it simply left his followers full of fear and amazement—but, as for Paul, the actual meetings with the one they had seen dragged off to execution. (For further detail, see Beare, *Gospel According to Matthew*, 542.)

3. *Ibid.*, 499.

4. *Ibid.*, 539.

5. Peake, *Commentary on the Bible*, 723.

GREEK AND JEWISH ROOTS OF THE ORTHODOX VIEW

1. See Cupitt in *Myth of God Incarnate*, 133.

2. Examples cited by Young, *ibid.*, 114, 115. In this chapter I am particularly indebted to Young and to Charles Talbert, "The Myth of the Descending-ascending Redeemer in Mediterranean Antiquity," *New Testament Studies* 22, 418ff.

3. Young in *Myth of God Incarnate*, 116.

4. *Ibid.*, 102. For further pagan parallels, see Sir James Frazer, *The Golden Bough*, abridged ed. (London: Macmillan, 1950), especially Chapter 7, "Incarnate Human Gods."

5. Talbert, "Myth of the Descending-Ascending Redeemer," 429.

6. Young in *Myth of God Incarnate*, 103.

7. Talbert, "Myth of the Descending-Ascending Redeemer," 429.

8. *Ibid.*, 430.

9. *Ibid.*, 440.

JESUS FROM NOW ON

1. *Book of Common Prayer*, 707.

2. *Heaven and Hell*, 18ff.

3. Edward Schillebeeckx, *God Is New Each Moment* (New York: Seabury, 1983), 26.

4. *Ibid.*, 22.

5. *Ibid.*

6. Stewart R. Sutherland, *God, Jesus, and Belief* (Oxford: Basil Blackwell, 1984), 163ff.

7. I agree entirely with Don Cupitt's point that a fresh understanding of Jesus will have the same liberating effect on the Church at large that modern scholarship has had on the Bible: "Just as a 'deabsolutized' scripture is of infinitely greater religious value than a flat oracle of fundamentalism, so a 'deabsolutized' Jesus can be recognized as revealing God to us in much more complex ways than the Christ of Chalcedon" (*Myth of God Incarnate*, 141).

8. Schillebeeckx, *God Is New Each Moment*, 43.

9. *Ibid.*

SELECTED READINGS

Barrett, C. K. *Jesus and the Gospel Tradition*. Philadelphia: Fortress, 1968.

Beare, F. W. *The Gospel According to Matthew*. New York: Harper and Row, 1981.

Boff, Leonardo. *Church: Charism and Power*. New York: Crossroads, 1985.

———. *Jesus Christ Liberator: A Critical Christology for Our Time*. Maryknoll, N.Y.: Orbis, 1978.

Carpenter, Humphrey. *Jesus*. Oxford: Oxford University Press, 1980.

Cullman, Oscar. *The Christology of the New Testament*. Rev. ed. Philadelphia: Westminster Press, 1980.

———. *The Johannine Circle*. London: SCM Press, 1976.

Fiorenza, Elisabeth Schüssler. *Bread Not Stone: The Challenge of Feminist Biblical Interpretation*. Boston: Beacon Press, 1984.

Guignebert, Charles. *Jesus*. Translated by S. H. Hooke. New Hyde Park, N.Y.: University Books, 1956.

Hick, John, ed. *The Myth of God Incarnate*. Philadelphia: Westminster Press, 1978.

Howes, Fred. *This Is the Prophet Jesus*. Marina del Rey, Cal.: Devorss, 1982.

Kümmel, Werner G. *The New Testament: The History of the Investigation of Its Problems*. Translated by S. M. Gilmour and H. C. Kee. London: SCM Press, 1978.

Küng, Hans. *Infallible? An Inquiry*. New York: Doubleday, 1971.

———. *On Being a Christian*. London: Collins, 1977.

Lindars, Barnabas. *Jesus Son of Man*. Grand Rapids, Mich.: Eerdmans, 1984.

McKinght, Edgar V. *What Is Form Criticism?* Philadelphia: Fortress, 1969.

Murphy, Cullen. "'Who Do Men Say That I Am?' Interpreting Jesus in the Modern World." *Atlantic* 258 (December 1986).

Ogden, S. M. *Christ without Myth*. New York: Harper and Row, 1961.

Perrin, Norman. *The Kingdom of God in the Teaching of Jesus*. London: SCM Press, 1963.

Robinson, J. M. *The New Quest of the Historical Jesus*. London: SCM Press, 1959.

Robinson, John A. *Honest to God*. Philadelphia: Westminster Press, 1963.

Ruether, Rosemary Radford. *Faith and Fratricide: The Theological Roots of Anti-Semitism*. New York: Harper and Row, 1974.

———. *Sexism and God Talk: Toward a Feminist Theology*. Boston: Beacon Press, 1983.

Schillebeeckx, Edward. *God Is New Each Moment*. New York: Seabury, 1983.

———. *Jesus—An Experiment in Christology*. New York: Seabury, 1979.

Schweitzer, Albert. *The Quest of the Historical Jesus*. New York: Macmillan, 1968.

Sheehan, Thomas. *The First Coming: How the Kingdom of God Became Christianity*. New York: Random House, 1986.

Stackhouse, Reginald. *The God Nobody Knows*. Toronto: Anglican Book Centre, 1986.

Stewart, Desmond. *The Foreigner: A Search for the First Century Jesus*. London: Hamish Hamilton, 1981.

Sutherland, Stewart R. *God, Jesus, and Belief*. Oxford: Basil Blackwell, 1984.

Wikenhauser, Alfred. *New Testament Introduction*. London: Herder and Herder, 1963.

INDEX